WHAT PEOPLE SAY
ABOUT THIS BOOK . . .

*Dedicated
to the
One Light
Shining in the Multicolored Lamps
of all Humanity*

SECRETS

A Practical Guide
to
Undreamed-of Possibilities

SECRETS
A Practical Guide to Undreamed-of Possibilities
By Christina Thomas

Publisher:

Chela Publications
977 Seminole Trail, Suite 308
Charlottesville, VA 22901 • USA
(804) 961-2960

First Paperback Edition 1989
Printed in the United States of America
Second Printing November 1989

Library of Congress Cataloguing in Publication Data
Thomas, Christina
  SECRETS
  A Practical Guide to Undreamed-of Possibilities

1. Self-Help
2. Psychology
3. New Age
4. Title

ISBN#0-9622119-0-7

 2 3 4 5 6 7 8 9 0

Cover Art: "Blue Drift" by Thomas Canny

CONTENTS

"St. Thomas"
pen and ink drawing by William Massey Thomas

ACKNOWLEDGMENTS

There are many people to whom I am grateful

My Beloved Parents, J. C. King and Bonnie Hardin King, for believing in me and in this book.

Sister Shanti, the Angel of Light who is a channel of love, wisdom and guidance in my life.

Julie, my littlest angel, for choosing me as your mother.

To those who helped with suggestions and editing of various manuscripts, especially Carol Risher and Shelley Phillipy.

Nathan Hoffman, for loving help and expertise in typesetting. Jan Tober, Anna Karg, Allen Hahn, Francis X. Maguire, Peggy Burkan, Dr. Frank Alper, Phil Laut, Grace Morris, Betty Hutto, Sharon Gary, Carmen Bucci, Tim and Danielle Heath and Marshall Thurber for love, enlightenment and encouragement.

My clients and workshop participants: I learn so much with you!

A Letter to My Readers

"The years of anxious searching in the dark, with their intense longing, their alternations of confidence and the final emergence into the light — only those who have experienced it can understand it."   Albert Einstein

People who have lived through near-death experiences often report that on "returning to life" they feel a sense of mission. I, too, have felt that sense of mission, that there was a definite and specific purpose for my life.

From early childhood, I was aware of a divine presence, aware of how energy permeates everything and aware that sometimes the words people used did not match the energy I felt emanating from them! I knew, for instance, when one person spoke the truth while another did not. I suspect that most young children have these abilities but, unlike many people, I did not lose the memory of them or the ability to feel these energies. I have always had a burning desire to understand the meaning of life, how the Universe works and the purpose of life on this planet.

My family attended the Pentecostal church. As I grew, I continued to feel the deep, personal inner connection with Spirit — but I also took on some of the fear and condemnation which often seems an inevitable part of the judgmental orientation of that sect. My family never fully adopted the fanaticism and blind following that some members exhibited. Fortunately, common sense and reason also had a place.

7

When I was 17 years old, I experienced the first big disillusionment I can recall. Not unlike some of the church scandals of recent years, the pastor of our church engaged in some behavior which violated his role as a church leader and as a result, my family and several other families withdrew. I had placed great faith in him and this experience destroyed that faith; worse, my faith in the beliefs was shaken and they had been an important framework in my life. The foundation on which I had stood was now badly damaged and I did not know how to repair it. I had based my life on the integrity of that church and clergyman; when they collapsed, so did part of my inner structure. I felt shattered, wounded and catapulted away from my familiar world into an outer space of existential despair!

As painful months passed by, I began to notice that although the outer structure of church ritual was gone from my life, the inner connection with Spirit remained as vibrantly alive as ever. One day I had an unforgettably powerful, numinous experience: In the midst of painful inner turmoil, I was searching for the meaning of the whole hurtful episode, viewing it as some terrible mistake, when suddenly I heard an inner voice, which felt like the voice of God: "Do not be concerned about mistakes! The only mistake you are making is that you have looked to other people for direction and I gave you the way to contact me directly."

At that moment, something within me shifted. I felt myself let go of the past and move into the aliveness of the present moment. I began to realize that the new direction my life had taken without my conscious consent contained some order and purpose after all. Since that time I have felt truly comfortable only when I have trusted my own inner guidance. Needless to say, I came to accept that the traumatic turn of events had really served to move me from a narrow place out into a much bigger world. It was really an incredible blessing!

So I was finally sailing my ship on open waters, looking back less, but I still had no idea where I was going. Over the next several years, I began opening to many new experiences. I felt like an alien from a spaceship here on Earth on assignment but I could not remember what the mission was. I would sometimes walk out under the stars, look up into the velvety darkness and literally plead for a response. The aliveness of the presence in the atmosphere and all of nature felt almost tangible to me but no response came — only a mute silence that left me in an agony of isolation. I often took it personally and wondered if there was something wrong with me. I didn't feel at home on Earth but I couldn't make contact with my "Mother Ship!" I seemed unable to escape this desperate searching for a reunion that constantly eluded me, piercing my heart. Try as I may to embrace life fully, inside me this pervasive sadness and longing never ceased.

I went on looking everywhere for "home", a spiritual context in which I could feel safe and find refuge from the disorientation I felt. Although the old values I discarded were ones I no longer could embrace, their departure left an empty void. To replace them, I hoped to find new values I could hold onto without sacrificing my aliveness. What I ultimately discovered was that once I left the "small room" I had occupied in conscious-ness, I never again would find another small room in which I would want to live. The choice was between living enthusiastically in an open attitude of discovery and adventure, or of compromising my sense of alive-ness for the sake of security— not really an option at all in my view. The parameters of my mind had expanded

9

so much that, despite my security needs, I finally accepted living in large, open spaces which kept opening to ever larger open spaces.

It was scary at times. I didn't know anyone who had ever travelled this road successfully; I had no model to follow. Certainly I knew people who had departed from the church life as I had known it, but it appeared they never subsequently achieved a healthy, balanced life, which I felt sure would include physical health, work satisfaction, psychological integration, harmonious relationships with self and others, and spiritual peace. All those elements were natural in a whole person, it seemed to me, and were part of my birthright. I already had some of them, but I lacked others and I wanted them all. I did not always know what was "right" for me, but often I knew what wasn't! So in trial-and-error fashion, I just kept taking each step and checking inside myself to see if something felt right for me. It was like looking for vital, missing puzzle pieces, checking each to see if it fit.

I would find something that was helpful and encouraging: Joel Goldsmith's books on meditation, the wisdom of Gandhi, the study of astrology - and feel propelled forward. These served me but did not provide that "something else" I was seeking. At other times I would feel frustrated and unsure of where I was going. At all times, though, I had an unwavering conviction that if I were honestly searching for truth, God would not let me go too far off the track so it was safe to keep searching. Living with both faith and doubt, my mind barraged me with questions: "What am I looking for? Does it even exist? If so, why haven't I met anyone else who seems to be looking for it?" But I could not stop searching.

It was finally in October 1971 that all the restless searching led me to a most important discovery: I heard the name of Paramahansa Yogananda for the first time. That very day I somehow knew my search was over, for I felt electrified, as though struck by a lightning bolt! For the next two weeks, his name resounded over and over in the background of my awareness like a broken record. I practically isolated myself, laughing and crying in an ecstatic relief beyond description. I had finally found my path and the recognition was unmistakable! I did not care that I may have appeared a little crazy. All I felt was joy and boundless love for everyone and everything!

My awareness began to shift to another level; a world where something essential had always been missing now suddenly made sense to me. I understood the essence of many things I did not understand before. It was clear to me that the only thing that mattered was love. And I perceived that everything is made of love: the whole Universe, all of creation, all human beings (which, in that state, appear as one whole residing in separate bodies like so many ladles full of soup all taken from the same pot). The boundaries of my separate identity dissolved in a sea of love. Everything is simple in this state of consciousness: There is only love!

On discovering my spiritual path, daily meditation became a very important part of life. Through that process, I have experienced an expansion that tells me there is no limit to the possibilities of consciousness. I experience that wherever I go in the world, I am at home. I recognize people of every race and creed as my family and have a knowingness that all paths lead to God. The safety I now feel is greater than I ever knew in the "small room" I left. It comes from the inner connection with Spirit, which was always there but which I had to learn to trust again, after having unwittingly abdicated some of my power to the authority of organized religion.

Soon after the experience in expanded consciousness described above, I got into my car which had been left unlocked in the parking lot of my apartment building. On the floor was an old, well-worn blue book, which I had never seen before. I reached for it, held it to the light to see the faded title, and gasped when I read:

Cosmic Consciousness! Although I never before had heard of either the book or the author, no subject on Earth was of greater interest to me! I had just finished reading Yogananda's "Autobiography of a Yogi," and begun a study of the Self-Realization Lessons, all of which mentioned Cosmic Consciousness so frequently as the goal of the meditating devotee. Where did this book come from? How did it get into my car? I inquired around but no one had ever seen it before. To this day I have no answers to those questions. But I am grateful for this gift and treasure the book as a priceless possession. I have read it a number of times and mention it here because it has had a profound impact on me. Originally published in 1901, it is now in print again. It has provided insight and clarity about what is occurring in consciousness today, not only to me but to many others, as the spiritual vibration of Mother

Earth quickens and increasing numbers of people experience the higher levels of consciousness described in the book.

In early 1972 I enrolled in a workshop, which was my initial training in the use of the Alpha brain-wave concentration technique. The joy and peace that had already begun to fill my interior life with the advent of meditation now augmented, as I learned techniques for reaching the Alpha level and utilizing it to achieve many very practical, day-to-day goals and solutions. I chose specific concentration experiments and tested them out in practical ways in my business and personal life, achieving clear results that could not ordinarily have been expected. I began sharing some of these methods with other people, most of whom were avowed skeptics. At times we would tackle an "impossible" situation with the attitude that "there is nothing to lose," and reap positive results. My initial emotional and intuitive response to the Alpha training had been resoundingly positive. Now the results of my experiments provided "real-world" corroboration: these techniques really worked!

I realized then that use of more of the mind and brain, easily accomplished with Alpha Concentration, worked far better than the use of logic and reasoning alone, and decided to join with the instructor to present the training to greater numbers of people. Use of these techniques truly became a way of life for me.

Having laid the groundwork for reaching my goals, I could more easily release ordinary concerns and devote all my meditation time to seeking pure communion with the divine, which is the true purpose of meditation. The two techniques of meditation and concentration thus worked well for me in combination, helping me to achieve more balance, peace and success

13

in my life. Two major pieces of my puzzle had fit into place. I was uncovering the secrets I had been seeking for so long!

In 1981 I moved to Encinitas, California, to live near the Self-Realization Ashram founded by Yogananda. It was in California that I discovered my third major puzzle piece, which is the technique of connected breathing (also called rebirthing). In my very first connected breathing session, I re-experienced my own birth and many feelings difficult to articulate. But I felt so different somehow that it was like I had suddenly become more awake.

I have since realized that usually one becomes aware that a suppression exists only after it has been cleared and integrated. It is like removing dark glasses you forgot you were wearing; suddenly everything looks lighter! I soon understood from my inward experiences that it was no longer necessary to carry around old feelings such as anger, guilt or hurt from the past in the form of suppressions. I was learning to breathe through them quickly, allowing them to integrate. Troublesome emotions which formerly could have bogged me down for days, draining my energy and distracting me away from full participation in each present moment, now could be dealt with in a wholesome, effective manner in a few hours and, sometimes, even in a few minutes! I had discovered another secret!

I recognized the great value of Connected Breathing as a tool for the cleansing and healing of the physical, emotional and psychological dimensions of a person. A priceless God-given tool designed into each human for clearing suppressions of negative energy, Connected Breathing leads to a greater experience of love on both a personal and spiritual level. After a year and a half of my own rebirthing process, my life was immeasurably enriched once again. Desiring to share my discoveries with others, I received training to be a professional rebirther. Now, along with my private rebirthing practice, I also conduct workshops to teach to others the universal principles which have proven to be so liberating in my own life. I feel such reward when another person experiences the awakening to the Higher Self that I cannot describe it. And this occurs frequently with rebirthing. If I were a billionaire, I would still do this work out of sheer joy!

Today I experience more love and freedom in my life than I ever dreamed of when I began my search. I believed in random happenings then, in fate or luck, which could be controlled perhaps. I no longer believe that anything is truly random. With expanded vision, one can see the orderly, magnificent intelligence at work in the universe and realize that we are in very good hands. In spite of all our fears, mistakes and misguided efforts, we are being guided back toward our home of limitlessness and love. We can delay our reunion with Spirit, but can hardly miss it altogether.

In your quest for wholeness, you must discover and embody your own missing pieces. Only you can choose them but sooner or later, each evolving person will require support in transformation. I have included the secrets which have contributed to my experience of wholeness. They may serve you in your journey, too, or at least lead you to some of your own discoveries. It is my heart's desire that this book will serve you.

Namaste,

Christina

1

Undreamed-of Possibilities!

" There is no limit to the unfolding of oneself."
Rabindranath Tagore

Do you recall the story of Aladdin and the magic lamp? He discovered that, when he rubbed the lamp, a genie would appear and grant him all his desires, whether for love, wealth, power or whatever. Because it would produce any wish, including some he might regret, Aladdin probably realized pretty quickly that it was wise to exercise discrimination and responsibility in the use of his magic lamp. Like many people, you may have daydreamed about having such a genie of your very own and it's no wonder, for you really do have such a magical, powerful helper. It is your mind. And like Aladdin, to achieve your desires, you need to learn exactly how to use it.

It comes as no surprise, then, to learn that the word "genie" is derived from the Latin word "genius," but you may be surprised to discover that the primary definition of genius is "guardian spirit." And we are discovering that the inner mind is exactly that. Connecting with this "genius," which is really an aspect of your higher mind, will infuse your life with power, happiness, energy and meaning almost beyond imagination. It has the power to bring into your experience undreamed-of possibilities!

So if each of us has this genius lying latent within the inner mind, why it is that so few people are truly realizing their goals and living their dreams. Why do most people fall so far short of their potential?

One of my favorite stories is about an eagle's egg that fell into a barnyard and landed in a chicken pen. The eaglet hatched out and was raised by the chickens. And since the only experience he had was that of chickens, he thought he *was* a chicken! One day a fox raided the chicken pen and the eaglet sat on the ground and was devoured along with the chickens. Now if he had had any idea of his real capabilities, he would have spread his mighty wings and flown away! His mistaken idea of his nature and abilities was fatal to him. So we are finding that it's not what we are but what we think we are that makes the difference in our life experience!

It is easy to understand, then, that if you go around thinking that you are a chicken, you are going to behave differently and attract different experiences than if you know you are an eagle. It would be a stretch for a chicken to fly over the barn, but an eagle is designed to soar high above the mountains just because he was born an eagle. And you were born to function at a much higher level; you are designed that way. When you learn how to work effectively with the genius or guardian spirit of your mind, you begin drawing on its power and energy to become the person you desire to be and, like a magnet, attract whatever you want in your life.

What we human beings usually do is attempt to work hard to reach this goal or that and to acquire this possession or that, without realizing that those things are not the prize we are seeking. What we are really after is the feeling of happiness that we think we will have when we get all those things. So why is it that it seldom ever seems to work that way? You reach a long-sought goal and what happens? Suddenly, there's another goal right out there in front of you! And sooner or later you begin to feel like the donkey following the carrot that is tied to his hat!

Why? What is going on? Eventually we begin to question our approach and realize that we have it all backwards! We are busy trying to fix the outside (our lives in the physical world) so the inside (feeling experience) will feel good. And it doesn't work that way. Certainly it is important to prepare ourselves in every way possible to function well in the external world but after we have done that, we still have to harmonize the inside, and then the outside will reflect that harmony. We see this sadly exhibited when a person has abundant material success, a prestigious position and a fine family, but still wrecks his life because he does not know how to find peace within.

Your Life is Your Mirror
Your life experiences are just reflecting back to you the state of your consciousness, but if you are not aware of that, you will often become upset with the results. You will tend to work harder at changing the outer world when it is really the inner world that is causing the outer — just a reflection. Now think about how you use a mirror. Do you want your mirror to show you how you really look (so you can take care of any corrections or improvements you wish to make) or do you want it to show you what you want to see (in which case you might go out among other people with spots on your clothing!) You can look at those spots and feel angry at the mirror or you can be grateful that you have such a good mirror to let you know what you want to clean up before you proceed any further!

I had a powerful experience wherein I felt truly grateful for a situation which I could have perceived as unpleasant. I conducted The Firewalk in Memphis, Tennessee, the heart of the Bible Belt. On the following Sunday The Commercial Appeal, a Memphis newspaper, ran a story about that Firewalk on the front page, showing a large photo of one of the participants boldly and fearlessly walking across the burning coals! (That article is reprinted in this book.) Needless to say, it attracted plenty of attention. A few days later, I appeared on a talk show to discuss The Firewalk; listeners were invited to phone in and the switchboard was bombarded with calls.

A little more of my background will help to communicate my feelings about this experience: Born on a farm in Tennessee and raised there until I was 10 years old, I am well acquainted with the Bible Belt culture. The fundamentalist beliefs, unfortunately, teach followers to be fearful and not open to something new. Because of that, I was aware before I agreed to lead The Firewalk in Memphis, that I had to deal with the residue of my own fears of being judged and condemned by those who might not understand the true purpose of The Firewalk, which is to help people learn how to face fear in a healthy, effective way and to discover that each of us has a form of inner guidance on which we can rely!

Sure enough, there were some calls from frightened, closed-minded folks accusing me of "doing the devil's work", however, even while we were on the phone, I was thinking and feeling as follows: "Isn't it wonderful for this person to verbalize the last threads of that old fearful belief that I have carried around at an unconscious level all these years? This person is really serving me and helping me to get clear, whether he realizes it or not. I am so glad to be able to allow it to become fully conscious now so it will have no more power!" I felt so grateful for the opportunity being given me to heal that limiting belief.

Because I know that nothing can happen in my life without my putting out a call for it to come along, I was able to deal with the situation with no bad feelings of any kind and, of course, I handled the call easily because I felt calm and relaxed about it.

It is a momentous awareness when you realize that what you are experiencing in your life is a reflection of the state of your consciousness. And that includes both what you know you believe consciously and, even more so, what you believe unconsciously! And now you may be wondering how can you change a thought or belief if you don't even know you have it in the first place. Believe it or not, using appropriate tools or techniques, it is fairly easy to discover what thoughts and beliefs make up your programming and to begin changing them.

Model for Wholeness

Everyone is a seeker. We are all looking for something, whether more money, more love, freedom from pain, or inner peace. It seems as though we need something from outside to complete us, when what we are really looking for is wholeness within ourselves. But how do you start becoming more whole? How do you find a missing element when you have no idea where to begin looking or even what it is? A map is needed for this journey in consciousness, an overall context which can remain stable enough to allow the inner contents to begin shifting and transforming. The four methods included in this book may provide that map for you as they have for me.

Today, increasing numbers of "New Age" teachers, books and organizations seem to lump together everything from ancient Oriental spiritual practices, like the time-tested physical postures of Hatha Yoga to an individual trance channeler offering every kind of advice from marital counsel to questionable stock market recommendations! Unless one already has a sound, healthy identity, it can be very confusing!

And, indeed, in work with individuals and groups over the past few years, I have observed frequently that in the area of consciousness, many seekers are truly confused. Groping in the dark, many are ignorant of even basic distinctions. To go from New York to California, it works best to take transportation heading west. It's not wrong to get on a southbound bus but it won't take you to your chosen destination! And in your search for the elements that will bring you to wholeness, you need to have a sense of where you are and where you want to go.

Likewise, when a dietician plans a menu, she will include foods from several groups which combine well with each other to make up a nutritious, balanced meal. Unaware of the overall goal of nutrition, however, one might choose only a beverage and three desserts, neglecting the essentials of entree and vegetables. Sometimes a dessert looks most appealing, but is totally lacking in nutritive value. In selecting your menu for wholeness, it is equally important to include balanced, integrating elements which truly nourish you.

As with a roadmap or a menu, it is important to use discrimination in choosing those elements. The model for wholeness embodied in this book can provide a context, a map to help you make vital distinctions and intelligent choices along the way.

It is not my intent to present here an exhaustive treatise on any of these four methods, but rather to introduce them in the context of interrelated parts of a whole, mentioned above. Further, deeper study of each of these methods will support your maturity in the disciplines. In the Recommended Reading section, you will find books for further study. And in the section called The Aquarian Network, I have included a listing of caring professionals and organizations. By contacting those of your choice, you may find further information and skilled, caring support in the chosen discipline, as you continue your journey in consciousness.

As already stated, the four effective methods which are the focus of this book offer a balanced menu for a healthy inner life. My experience of them over many years is that they, indeed, comprise a model for wholeness. Each method addresses a different, vital area of human need. One method is not intended to substitute for the work of the other. Each is best used in its specific area of application, although because all is consciousness work, there is sometimes an overlapping. Each works well alone or combined with one or more of the other methods. These methods contain the secrets which can transform your life at all levels. As you begin to practice and integrate them into your life, you will understand much more about them in an intuitive way. At the beginning, however, I suggest that you need not concern yourself with attempting to mentally understand how and why the techniques operate as they do within the gestalt of the human person.

These techniques are all vital parts of my experience. I practice them; I live them; my life has been transformed by them. So I am writing from a perspective of knowingness about how they actually work, rather than mere belief.

I have learned that there is wisdom in approaching anything and everything with a scientific attitude. For instance, "I will make no judgment about this until I have tried it out in the laboratory of my own experience" appeals to keen intelligence more than judging the efficacy of a thing without giving it a true test in your own life. And so I urge you to apply these methods and then decide if they have value for you. The four methods are:

1. **Alpha Concentration**
2. **Connected Breathing/Rebirthing**
3. **Meditation**
4. **Affirmation**

You may use these methods singly or in any combination, depending on what you wish to achieve; each supports the other and augments the energy directed into your life. I have found that the best applications for these methods are:

1. **Alpha Concentration:** Use to focus your attention and your energy on those day-to-day elements you wish to bring into your life experience. I use this method primarily in the mundane world, i.e., specific goal achievements.

2. **Connected Breathing/Rebirthing:** Use to clear and integrate the suppressed, negative energy, including the physical, emotional and psychological dimensions, which has accumulated since before your birth. This constitutes the bath which will cleanse you and prepare you for higher levels of experience on both the mundane and higher dimensions.

3. **Meditation:** Use to focus your attention away from the mundane world (always somewhat unreliable) to the peace of the higher perception of God (always reliable and not dependent on outer circumstances). Sometimes, the most effective place to start is Meditation because it will quickly prepare your mind to be even more receptive and ready to get on with your life. Meditation, alone, would ultimately heal every area of your life, however, this healing process can be greatly speeded up and supported by the other methods.

4. **Affirmation:** Use to re-program your thoughts and beliefs at first the subconscious level and ultimately reaching into the vast regions of superconsciousness. Regardless of which method(s) you choose to begin working with, it is helpful to support that work with Affirmation.

You may begin with any of these methods but all are so powerful and effective that you will benefit most if you incorporate all of them into your life. May this book help you open to the guardian spirit of your higher mind and to the energy, happiness and meaning that flow into your life when you have made that connection.

2

The Secret of Concentration

*"Within a couple of decades, it will be widely accepted
that inner conscious awareness is a cause of reality
in the universe and in our daily lives."*
                    Dr. Willis Harmon
                    Stanford University

Concentration is the process of using your thoughts
or imagination in conjunction with your feelings to
create whatever you want in your life. Specifically, we
will discuss in detail how to concentrate in a relaxed
way when the brainwaves slow down to what science
calls the Alpha brain-wave level, which is naturally a
little slower than ordinary waking levels,

First, let us look more deeply into what actually
comprises the process of true concentration. Scientific
studies have shown that when most human beings
think, they are seeing pictures or images in their mind's
eye. How often have you heard someone say, "I just
can't picture that!" or "I can just see you doing this."
So you are already using visual imagery much of the
time, however, this alone, does not create a response.
You are not always creating when you are visualizing.
When does mental and visual imagery become creative
and dynamic? What causes it to become reality in your
life? It is when you are experiencing strong feelings <u>and</u>
visualizing your thoughts that you are creating your
reality.

It is your natural ability as a human being to form
the fundamental creative energy of the universe into

the objects you have strong feelings about and imagine vividly. You are the potter; the universal energy is the clay. Combining your thoughts and images with your intense feelings forms the pottery that makes up your life experience, both tangible and intangible. There is nothing new or even unusual about Alpha-level Concentration. This book will simply take you in step-by-step fashion to begin creating your life more consciously out of your choices.

You were formed in the womb and born into this world as a powerful creature of nature; immediately began the process of shaping your life to fit into your family, culture, religion, etc. You began acquiring not only a mountain of records and statistics, being footprinted, named and numbered, but you began absorbing beliefs, biases, prejudices and limitations that would define and differentiate you from the other babies born the same day in the same place. Before you could even begin to know what a belief is, you had an entire belief system in place in your magnificently creative brain and nervous system. And along with your family name and other legacies, you inherited concepts in the form of beliefs that accompany you throughout life, frequently limiting your view of yourself and your world. Of course, these were handed to you in ignorance, just the way your parents and grandparents received them before you. But they keep you from living your life fully, from experiencing joyful, alive relationships. These beliefs keep you from creative, satisfying work, optimum health, abundant prosperity — the very stuff of life!

A very important key for many people at this point in opening themselves to a greater experience of life, is to realize that they can continue to love their parents, their family, their culture *without holding onto beliefs*

26

that no longer work for them! They can let go of family belief systems and continue to love their families! They can view it in the same way they view a grade at school: one can complete fifth grade and leave it behind without finding any fault with it, taking along all the value and nourishment of the positive experiences and lessons learned.

Feeling is the Essential Ingredient

Once you understand the process of ridding yourself of old belief systems without judging or criticising either yourself or the old beliefs, you can embrace the next step joyfully: combining mental pictures with strong feelings to manifest your desires. With Alpha Concentration, you use your ability to make vivid mental pictures of what you want to manifest and stay with those mental pictures until you feel the feelings you will experience when those pictures are a reality in your physical world. Once you have the feeling experience you wish to manifest, then you continue to fuel it with the energy of your mental pictures *and* your strong feelings until the projection becomes actual reality, until you have the result of what you have been visualizing.

It is important to realize that thoughts or imagery alone, without feelings, will produce little or nothing for you. The feeling dimension is truly the fuel that will carry the rocket of your thought-pictures to the level of manifestation. If you go around seeing images of yourself as rich *but feeling poor,* you will more likely have additional experiences of being poor — you will reap the results of the feelings, not the images! If you honestly examine your own inner process, you will discover that when you are experiencing feelings about something, especially if they are strong feelings, your thoughts, images and self-talk are also involved. Therefore, repeating an affirmation or flashing an inner mental image that is the opposite of those feelings is really just "parroting" and, as such, will not activate the energy to create.

Because of this, it is the feeling tone that is more truly creative; if you really want to know what you are creating, observe what you are feeling. When feelings are coupled with thought images, it is as though egg and sperm have united. Potent new life begins forming for a birth to come when the appropriate gestation has been completed. And, just as it is unnecessary for your conscious mind to really understand the mystery of how a sperm unites with an ovum to begin forming a new baby, your conscious understanding of the mystical process of creating through visualization and feelings is unnecessary. All you need do is trust that if you follow these techniques, the principle will work for you.

You may choose a goal from any dimension of your life — from the physical, emotional, mental or spiritual levels. You might envision a home that is the epitome of all your dreams yet easily affordable. You may visualize work that will be so truly fulfilling that you would joyfully give yourself to it regardless of any need to produce income, or you might imagine a totally committed, fulfilling relationship that is mutually empowering to you and your mate. . . and any other dream you want. Napolean Hill aptly stated that "whatever the mind of man can conceive and believe, it can achieve!" And an easy, natural way to those achievements is to employ Concentration at the Alpha level.

Four Key Elements

There are four essential elements of Alpha-level Concentration:

1. FEELINGS. You must really desire what you are visualizing. The energy of the universe responds when you feel very strongly about your visual image. Those feelings act like a magnet attracting into your life more of the same thing you are imagining, and more of the kind of feelings you are already experiencing. It is appropriate and healthy to use your feelings of desire to achieve your goals.

2. VISUALIZATION. The better you can see your thought picture, the more effective your visualization will be. Clarity leads to power. When you know exactly what you want, you are far more likely to achieve it. See colors, shapes, sizes and dimensions as vividly as possible. Fill in the details exactly as you would do if you were placing an order for the item, realizing that you will get exactly what you describe. Much scientific work has shown that the imagery function of the brain is more universal and incessant than was formerly believed. Even among people who are blind since birth, apparently there is some visual imagining that occurs within the inner processes of the brain.

It is not important to "see" things at the inner level the same way you see with your physical eyes. The inner imaging may be experienced as a kinesthetic sensation or it may feel more like a "connection" with the thing you are visualizing. The vital ingredient is focused, undistracted attention on what you are creating in your thoughts. You can use Alpha Concentration successfully whether or not you consider yourself a visual person.

3. ACCEPTANCE. You must be willing to accept your good when it arrives. Although it makes no logical sense to the conscious mind, we sometimes will not allow ourselves to experience something if we have a thought or belief that it has come too easily or that we do not deserve it. You will only allow yourself to experience something if it is within the scope of your self image. (Your self image is not what you are but is the sum total of what you *think* you are.) The only way to be, do or have something that is beyond your present self image is to change your thoughts about yourself, thus expanding your self image.

4. THE "AS IF" ATTITUDE. You must reinforce your Alpha Concentration by adopting the feeling and attitude that you already have the thing you desire. This is often not easy to do but is essential if you are to succeed. Ask yourself, "How will I feel when this is already a reality in my life?" And then begin to feel those feelings now, knowing that thereby you are putting out a call for more of those same feelings. Remember that what you focus on increases so it is important to focus on your visualization and the accompanying feelings "as if" that were already the reality, and not on the way things may appear in your outer world right now. By continuing to play your role in the world while holding onto your new thought picture and good feelings, you create that thought picture as your outer reality.

Focus All Four Lenses

It is as though these four elements are lenses through which you view your world. In order to see clearly, you must line them all up. Then an intense focus of purpose will result, a focus which cannot fail to create what you desire in your life.

Relaxation is Essential

To effectively use Alpha Concentration to bring about changes in your life, you must relax deeply. Understanding a little of how the brain functions explains this vital requirement.

If you had an electroencephalograph (EEG) machine (which measures brain waves) attached to your head, you would see that when you are in a normal waking state of consciousness, the brain waves would fall into a relatively fast range of 14 to 21 cycles per second (cps) which is referred to as the Beta level. The Beta brain wave pattern shows up on the EEG graph as small, rapid, up-and-down lines.

There is not much fluctuation in the level of energy in or to the brain at this level. When you alter your state of awareness by relaxing deeply, your brain wave level slows down to the rhythm of about 7 to 14 cycles per second, which is called the Alpha level, or to about 4 to 7 cycles per second, which is called the Theta level. In these states, the EEG machine would show larger, slower brain wave patterns, indicating large fluctuations of energy in and to the brain.

It is *only* during these periods of large fluctuations in brain wave energy that re-programming occurs in the powerful biocomputer of your subconscious mind. In this relaxed state, your subconscious mind is open to receiving messages from your conscious mind. By forming clear messages and accompanying them with strong feelings, you will actually create what you want in your life easily and peacefully without effort, worry and struggle, without forcing things to happen. When you fully realize this truth, you begin to relax in your attitude toward yourself and your relationship to other people and the world!

Alpha is an Everyday Experience

It is very natural and easy to relax and enter the Alpha level. You experience it a number of times every day. As you awake from sleep, at times when you are quietly daydreaming, often when you are relaxed and listening to soft music, and on falling asleep, the brain waves automatically slow to the Alpha level. At the end of this chapter, detailed instructions for reaching the Alpha level are given. You may wish to record this in your own voice or have a friend read it to you so you can fully experience it. Or you may send for an audio cassette (entitled "Secrets") on which I have recorded this and other techniques and exercises with peaceful music to help you master the art of Alpha Concentration (see order form at the back of this book).

In the beginning, you may require several minutes to slow your consciousness down to the Alpha level. As you practice, however, you will be able to relax into Alpha quickly and easily. As with most skills, it works best in the beginning to take each step slowly, in sequence, learn it well, then once well-learned, speed up the process with no loss of quality.

What this means in addition is that you are developing the ability to relax at will, which is very recharging to your mind and body batteries. Much scientific research in recent years clearly shows that frequent, brief periods of relaxation greatly relieve stress and contribute to a sense of peaceful well-being.

So by relaxing deeply, you can use Alpha Concentration at any time. It is easy to use in the sleepy state when you first begin to awaken in the morning and again as you become drowsy when falling asleep at night. It is fine to do while lying down but if you tend to fall asleep, it is important to include other periods of Alpha Concentration during the day to make sure you have programmed your subconscious the way you want to!

After you learn to relax and enter the Alpha state quickly, you will find it helpful to use it often. An excellent technique is to use it at any time you feel anxiety. Instead of getting into the feeling of anxiety, you just stop, relax and shift into Alpha, and visualize what you want the way you want it and feel how good that feels.

I am not suggesting that you believe anything. I am recommending that you approach Alpha-level Concentration with an attitude of "let me find out if this will work for me." Approach it with a feeling of openness to discovering what is, without any prejudice or bias for having the result be this way or that. Then you will have the experience of "knowing" instead of "believing" these techniques to be true. To experience the scientific results of true Concentration is to experience the power of being connected to the entire universal support system in which we live. It is to discover that "I am not alone and I do not have to function alone. The Universe supports me with abundance in every area of my life." If you approach these techniques with an attitude of openness to discovering what is, you will experience enormous, beneficial changes beginning to occur in your life. If your experience is like mine, those changes will take you on a path of discovery beyond your fondest dreams.

Concentration at the Alpha level is a simple, powerful, natural technique; it works like magic, producing results without having to understand how you arrived at that result. It involves trusting the natural workings of the magnificent universe of which we are a vital part, and learning to trust the wisdom of the universe no matter what appears to be happening in the space we physically occupy at the moment.

The great master, Paramahansa Yogananda, once commented that if, when you saw a rose, you began examining its petals and trying to figure out what made it look and smell like a rose, that you would miss entirely the essence of the rose. But, of course, you know that you can enjoy the fragrance of the rose and its beauty without ever understanding how such exquisite perfection came into existence.

The very same thing applies to Alpha-level Concentration. In the beginning you may feel awestruck when you experience your images and feelings manifesting in your life experience; but soon you will allow it to be okay that your limited conscious mind does not understand how your heartfelt imagery becomes reality. You will begin to trust that vast part of yourself that is beyond the little conscious mind.

When this occurs, you will experience the peaceful awareness that you are allowing miracles to be created through you as a magnificient and powerful child of the universe. And your life will never be the same!

To understand how Alpha Concentration works, it is necessary to examine several universal principles.

The Material Universe is Made of Energy
Everything in creation had its birth in energy. When we are mentally attuned to that Universal En-

ergy, we begin to realize that everything in creation is a manifestation of that energy. Differences in the rates of vibration account for its varying expressions. Take as an example a solid object like a wooden table. Place it under a microscope and it appears less solid than with the naked eye — you now can see the spaces between the molecules. Step up the microscopic intensity and there appear still more spaces and less solid material. Use an electron microscope and the solid quality diminishes again, with a compensating increase of space. So what is matter? Not much of anything, except energy!

$E = mc^2$

Heralding the Aquarian Age like a brilliant metaphor, Einstein's famous equation - energy equals mass times the speed of light squared - opened to 20th-Century mankind the awesome power of the atom. Delineating the equivalence of mass (matter) and energy (light), leads to the awareness that the release of the energy of the atom is brought about via the annihilation of matter. The atom is the basic structure of the material plane, the lowest common denominator of energy (light) becoming matter. It becomes easier to realize, then, that the whole of creation, including the human, physical body, is really energy or light masquerading as matter. Our true essence is that we are light beings!

Paralleling this example of nuclear fission, we allow our material consciousness to die (be transformed) in order to be born to the more powerful energy state of a higher level of consciousness. As in the example of a caterpillar, what seems like death is really just that of one's limited expression surrendering its narrow boundaries to the higher life of a greater expression. All we lose are our limitations!

We have examples one after another that everything in our physical world is made of energy. The perception of an object, whether a tree or a wall or our physical bodies, is solid only because we perceive it to be solid. And, indeed, when we change our perception sufficiently, then we experience even physical properties as behaving differently.

The Firewalk is one of my favorite workshops because it is a perfect example of how changing one's thoughts and feelings causes a major and immediate shift in one's physical experience. At the beginning of The Firewalk workshop, the participants and I build a big bonfire using ordinary fireplace logs. When we light the fire, it is common for the participants to experience a lot of fear. The fire is very hot and feelings are usually very intense among the participants. Those intense feelings provide a great amount of energy for significantly shifting the beliefs of the participants during the next few hours. The workshop culminates in the experience of walking barefoot across burning coals that measure between 1,250 and 2,000 degrees Fahrenheit!

Your stove at home reaches only about 550 degrees at its hottest and just a fingertip's contact for a moment will produce a painful blister. But because of the ideas and feelings experienced during The Firewalk workshop, the mental, emotional and physical perception of the participants shift. Not only do I lead the way barefoot across those coals, but every participant who attempts to follow me walks across unharmed as well! They feel and see it differently and have a correspondingly different experience!

But how can it be that not only does The Firewalk participant feel no pain on walking across burning hot coals, but the bare flesh (which, according to physical law, normally blisters at well under 200 degrees Fahrenheit) obeys as well, producing no blisters or other effect? No one yet can answer that question; we do not know why it works this way. What is apparent is that when you alter your viewpoint sufficiently, the physical universe alters its behavior to align with your beliefs! A focused state of mind is the crucial variable.

Using your power of Concentration and visualization effectively, that is, making it dynamic by imbuing it with the energy of your strong feelings of desire and will power, enables you to materialize your thoughts in the material realm.

What You Focus on Increases!

Another universal principle is that whatever you place your attention on increases. Our thoughts and feelings operate in a fashion similar to a magnifying glass. It is as though your mind is a magic lens which, when focused in a concentrated manner with strong feeling, will multiply or increase the object of your attention.

Too often we use this universal law in a negative way, by worrying or feeling fearful about some imagined future event. At those times we are really placing an order for the experience we are worrying about or fearing! Simply stated, we attract whatever we focus on. Like attracts like. Although thoughts cannot be seen by our physical eyes, their power in the physical world is unmistakable.

Manifestation Follows Your Mental Blueprint

The relationship between thought and matter is very subtle. When we are using concentration in a dynamic way, we have a thought or idea and then imbue it with the intensity of our life force energy in the form of desire or strong willpower (or, negatively, fear). Whether the idea is as simple as planting a flower or as grand as writing an epoch novel, the idea must always precede the creation.

A builder follows the architect's design to build a house. An author has his central idea before beginning to write a book. A dressmaker follows a pattern to create a new garment. Inventions are the result of the materialization of human thought.

Your idea is just like those blueprints; it forms an image in the ether. When your idea is strong and sharply focused, it will begin to attract additional energy to itself like a magnet, much the way a fertilized cell begins attracting energy to form an embryo.

Whatever you send out returns to you multiplied. This is the law that whatever you give out you receive back, usually increased. In the Oriental cultures, it is called the law of Karma. In the Western world it is most often stated ". . .as you sow, so shall you reap." As a practical matter, what it means is that you will attract into your individual experience whatever you empower most with your thoughts, imagination and feelings. This works both negatively and positively. If you use your life force energy to create negative thought forms of jealousy, fear or greed, you will experience negative situations finding their way to your doorstep. And conversely, people who hold onto an intrinsic optimism about life attract positive results that often defy explanation! It is frequently a question of whether or not one sees the glass half empty or half full. Therefore, the more positive energy you mobilize, the greater will be the happy return on your energy investment.

Using Alpha Concentration

Many people attempt to achieve results in the realm of thought without succeeding, and perhaps give up without discovering the root cause of the failure. Positive thinking alone will not produce results for you. But those persons who visualize their thoughts very strongly with clear focus and accompanying intense feeling, are able to manifest those images in outward form. It requires a willingness on your part to become more alert and aware of your thoughts from moment to moment and undertaking a process of discovery to find out what works for you. It takes an openness to uprooting your own negative biases and replacing them with positive beliefs that will support your goals. Experiment with your thought life. Test out your strongest thoughts on your body to see if you can overcome some pain or area of physical weakness. Start small. When you have achieved success with that small project, you will be able to tackle a bigger chunk with the encouragement of a recent "win" to spur you on.

Initially, it is useful to have a notebook for your Alpha Concentration work and practice at specific times on specific projects, recording your efforts and results accurately. Be prepared for much self-discovery and expansion in your life. Simply beginning to use these techniques and validating for yourself in the laboratory of your own experience that the universal principles set forth here are, in fact, unfailing laws governing our world will create in your awareness more happiness, peace and aliveness than you can probably imagine.

Science has shown us that we ordinarily use a maximum of 10% of our capacity through our conscious minds. As you use the techniques contained in this book, you will find that they are becoming more automatic. You will find yourself using the techniques effortlessly, calling on more of the other 90% of your power and creativity, becoming more competent without having to know consciously how it is happening.

Eventually you will discover that the old method of functioning has given way to a new order in your life, an order in which you create your own life of happiness and fulfillment from your conscious choice. The more you visualize with deep concentration and relaxation, the clearer will be your inner realization of your true identity: that you are not your body, mind or personality, but that you are the energy behind them.

By using these techniques, you will begin accepting and exercising your power as a spiritual being. The whole universe is arranged to support your recall of who you really are. Practicing these techniques will allow you to manifest the things you want and will help you to grow on every level.

An Exercise in Concentration

You may wish to make a tape recording of this exercise in your own voice so that all you need do is relax and follow the instructions. Or have a friend read it to you, slowly and quietly, perhaps with soft music in the background.

1. Sit or lie down comfortably. Take a few deep breaths and begin allowing your whole body to relax completely from head to toe. Tense and then relax each body part in succession. Finally, let your toes just flop outward in complete relaxation.

2. Now inhale deeply and as you exhale, visualize the color red and the number 7. Take another deep breath and as you exhale, visualize the color orange and the number 6. Take another deep breath and as you exhale, visualize the color yellow and the number 5. Take another deep breath and as you exhale, visualize the color green and the number 4. Take another deep breath and as you exhale, visualize the color blue and the number 3. Take another deep breath and as you exhale, visualize the color purple and the number 2. Take another deep breath and as you exhale, visualize the color violet and the number 1.

You are now at Level 1, a deeper, more restful, more powerful level than before. Continue to breathe in and out naturally as you mentally repeat the following positive thoughts and ideas which will quickly manifest in the outer expression of your life as better health, more prosperity and greater happiness.

"Everything I touch turns to success."

"I am always applying myself in ways that make me and others happy."

"I love to eat healthy foods in just the right amount for my perfect body weight."

"I am continually using my mind and emotions in ways that call upon more of the genius of my higher mind."

"I am completely relaxed and completely alert as I apply myself to the tasks I choose."

"I am efficient, creative and productive in all my endeavors."

In fact, "Every day in every way, I am getting better and better."

Take a few more deep breaths, just allowing the exhalation to fall away without controlling it. And now

41

we will begin to move from Level 1 back to Level 7, as we count up slowly:

Continue breathing and move up, now, from Level 1 up to Level 2. Breathe in and on the exhale, move up from Level 2 to Level 3. Take another breath and move up from Level 3 to Level 4. Remember, at the count of 7 to open your eyes.

Take another breath and move from Level 4 to Level 5. Breathe in again and on the exhalation, move up from Level 5 to Level 6. Take another breath and as you exhale, move up from Level 6 to Level 7. Open your eyes, be wide awake, refreshed and in tune with life!

An audio cassette recording of this and other exercises is available from the publisher. Please refer to the Order Form at the back of this book or have your bookstore order for you.

3

Thought is Creative

"Mind is the creator of everything. If you cling to a certain thought with dynamic will power, it finally assumes a tangible outward form."
Paramahansa Yogananda

Today modern science is beginning to discover and investigate what ancient Eastern teachings have long promulgated: that thought is creative, that in fact your life is an "out-picturing" of your thoughts. You may well ask how this can be. "Surely I have not created my life as it is," you may object; "I would never choose this financial stringency or that illness or this loneliness!" A very important distinction here is that, of course, you do not *consciously* choose all the factors present in your life; as a matter of fact, most of the cause stems from the unconscious. But by becoming more aware of how this works, you can take the rudder of the ship of your life more consciously into your own hands, begin to create from choice and not continue as an uninformed actor in a play written through a process you do not understand. Let us examine specifically what that process is.

First, let us discuss exactly what is meant by "thought." It is really more accurate to state that thought is creative *when combined with feeling*. This is the part that many people leave out. It is no wonder, then, that their results are sometimes disappointing. Thought alone, often accompanied by visual images, represents the masculine energy (or sperm); when combined with the feminine energy of feeling (the egg), manifestation will occur in the physical dimension we call reality. Neither the sperm alone nor the egg alone will result in physical manifestation. But put them together and new life begins — new life in the form of reaching your goals, realizing your dreams — experiencing the appearance in your life of whatever you place your attention on when combined with the powerful energy of your feelings.

A little self-introspection will obviate that you are not your thoughts, but you are the thinker behind your thoughts — you are the one who chooses what thoughts to think. When I made this point in a workshop, one participant said, "But I only choose some of my thoughts; a lot of thoughts just pop into my head. Sometimes I don't even want to think about them. . ."

This seemingly automatic quality of thought is an illusion, just as movie film is really a series of still photographs which gives the illusion of motion when fed rapidly through a projector. With the techniques in this book, you will learn to make changes at the inner, most powerful level of mind and your outer world will change accordingly.

People sometimes doubt that the inner world really creates the outer world. But it is really just like changing the film in a movie projector: If you insert "Gone with the Wind" in the projector, there is no way you are going to see "The Wizard of Oz!" So if you do not like the movie on the screen of your life, you can change it only by changing your thoughts.

The ordinary person thinks 50,000 thoughts per day; a highly-evolved person perhaps ten times that number. Some of those are passing thoughts with little or no feeling, but many carry feelings of some intensity.

You need only to take upon yourself as an experiment the careful watching of all your thoughts and the conscious direction of them for a day or two to observe a remarkable change in your life and awareness. Most human beings run what would be equivalent to two or three movies at the same time, resulting in a cancelling-out effect. If you have a positive thought and also at the same time or later a negative one, it will result in a waste of energy, a cancelling out one of the other.

Consciousness follows attention. Where you place your attention, therefore, is of the utmost importance. Many things vie for your attention at almost every moment of the day, either in the external world and/or internally as we recall memories (often in a negative way, usually in the form of guilt), or into the future (usually fear and worry). Guilt and fear are very powerful emotions and, therefore, make the thoughts they are combined with very creative. Seen in this light, it becomes apparent that not only do these emotions bring you misery, they literally attract the very object of your fear! As Job said in the Old Testament, "The thing which I had greatly feared is come upon me. . ." (Job 3:25).

So how do you focus your attention and keep it focused to make the powerful laser of your mind manifest as you want? Making a list of goals you want to begin working toward and then allocating regular periods of concentration will assist you in bringing order and structure to your life, allowing you to create your life as you desire it to be, using scientific methods that have been proven in countless lives. But it is never good enough to take someone else's word on a subject that is truly important to you; if you really care about reaching your goals, if you really care about the quality of your life, you will be satisfied only with testing these principles in the laboratory of your own experience.

Decide to work on each goal in a specific way for an exact period of time. Keep a written record of your goals and the particular exercise you are utilizing to reach each goal.   Record your results clearly, systematically and honestly.   The shift in your belief will add fuel to the rocket of your future projects.

> *"There is nothing more potent than thought.*
> *Deed follows word and word follows thought.*
> *The world is the result of a mighty thought and*
> *where the thought is mighty and pure, the result*
> *is always mighty and pure."*
>
> *Mahatma Gandhi*

4

Creating What You Want

"This is what intelligence is:
paying attention to the right things."
Edward Hall

Realizing that consciousness follows attention, it becomes apparent that where you place your attention is of the utmost importance, for you will expand or multiply that element in your life experience. You can use Alpha-level Concentration to create whatever you choose.Included below are several exercises which will help you to begin incorporating these techniques into your life and give you a feeling for using the techniques easily.

Centering Exercise
This technique is very simple and very effective. It is helpful to use it morning and night. The idea is to align the energy along your spine and give you a sense of connectedness both to Earth and to your energy source. It will enable you to feel poised and centered with feet planted firmly on the ground.

Exercise:
1. Stand facing East with feet about 10 inches apart. Close your eyes and begin breathing deeply and slowly, connecting each inhale and exhale without pausing between breaths.

2. Inhale fully and imagine that the energy is moving from your tailbone upward along the spine toward the top of the head and as it moves upward silently repeat the words "I am." As the energy reaches the top of your head, begin exhaling, allowing the energy to move down over the nose and mouth and down the front of the body to the genital area.   As the energy is moving downward, mentally repeat your first name.

3. Repeat this inhalation with energy moving up the back of your spine and exhalation with energy moving down the front of the body for a total of three times. Each time you silently repeat, "I am _____." When you have completed the third round, just forget about your breath, allowing it to be natural and automatic.

4. Now visualize that in your abdomen there is a tiny sphere of light glowing very brightly. Imagine now that a beam of that light is travelling downward, down through your legs and out your feet down into the ground until the end of that beam is anchored at the very center of the Earth.   Leave that beam of light there.

5. Imagine that on the very top of your head is another little sphere of light, glowing brightly. Now send a beam of that light upward through the sky until the end of that beam reaches the very source of energy and light and love in the universe.   Imagine that a rainbow shower of light is being poured into the top of that beam and see it now travelling downward along the beam into the little sphere of light on your head. Visualize that it continues to travel downward through your body, connecting with the other sphere of light in your abdomen and on down to the very center of the Earth.

6. Realize that you are a clear channel of light that originates at the source and travels downward through your body to the very center of the Earth. Realize that wherever you go, you will be a channel of light and positive energy, benefitting everyone and everything in the vicinity of your consciousness.   The light is so omnipresent that it will flow through any channel that is

clear enough. And you are that clear channel now. Take a few more breaths and open your eyes, prepared to move about in your life grounded and centered in energy.

Because this visualization is very powerful, it is advisable to do the entire exercise only twice a day (morning and evening). If you wish to re-center yourself during the day, you may safely repeat this exercise, eliminating Step 6. (Sending the light upwards more often may tend to "space you out".)

Affirmation: I am a channel for the Infinite Light.

Creating Your Ideal Day

Select a goal that is fairly easy and use Alpha-level Concentration to accomplish it. This will provide you with confidence and faith for the more challenging concentration projects. For instance, you can program tomorrow to be an Ideal Day.

Exercise:

Find a quiet place and become very relaxed. Take a few deep breaths, visualize the spectrum of colors red, orange, yellow, green, blue, purple and violet. Turn your closed eyes slightly upward. See and feel yourself awaking at the perfect time tomorrow morning feeling vibrantly alive and with a sense of serenity, health and well-being. Feel the confidence and enthusiasm. See yourself arise and sit in meditation, morning exercise or whatever you choose to do first.

When ready, begin your bathing and grooming routine. As you proceed, notice how wonderful and warm the water feels during your bath and how balanced and relaxed you feel after your bath as you dry off. As you continue your grooming process, be aware that today you look radiantly alive as though the vibrant life force energy within you is clearly evident in your appearance. If you are a man, notice that shaving is smooth and comfortable. If you are a woman, notice that your hair behaves beautifully and looks better than you can ever remember; your makeup is soft and becoming to you. Your eyes shine with confidence, poise and love.

Get dressed in your favorite clothes for this occasion. Notice how well they fit, how attractive they look on you, how comfortable and easy to wear.

Proceed right on to your next chosen activity. Experience it in detail, creating it exactly the way you want it to be. Include the visual — have everything look exactly as you wish. Choose to feel at ease, confident, centered and powerful (and any other feelings you wish) in order to have exactly the feelings you want throughout the day. Observe that other people interacting with you throughout the day are positive, supportive, cooperative, harmonious, willing and even eager to assist you in every detail of your chosen goals and activities. Hear them speak to you exactly as you desire; even hear your favorite music at appropriate times throughout this day. You are creating your life so choose exactly what you want in every way. Continue your Concentration process visualizing your day exactly as you want it throughout the entire day until you retire at night and go to sleep.

Take a few more deep breaths and prepare to return to ordinary waking consciousness. Then just relax and allow events to flow.

Doing light connected breathing occasionally and staying relaxed throughout the day will facilitate the flow of your good toward you. Go lightly through the day and allow the flow.

At the end of your Ideal Day, take time to review your day, acknowledging yourself for creating the little miracles that will have occurred throughout the day. If there are areas where something did not develop as you programmed, review to see if you can determine if you need to change some aspect of your Concentration work.

For instance, are you sure you programmed congruently? Did part of you *not want* the outcome you visualized? Reviewing your day in slow motion can help you detect an error which might interfere with your desired results. Now use the information from your review to create an even more perfect Ideal Day exercise.

What Do You Want . . . Specifically?

Imagine walking up to an airline ticket counter and stating emphatically, "I do not want to go to San Francisco!" What would the ticket agent do? Right! Probably nothing at all! Now that scene seems ridiculous but how many times do we act similarly? To the question, "What do you want in your life?", many people will answer, "I don't want to live like this anymore!"

The point is that until we are clear about what we want in our experience, we are very unlikely to get it. To use Concentration or Affirmation effectively, you must know what it is you want, and the more clear and sharp the images, the more likely you are to manifest it in the outward world. If you do not already know what you want, then obviously one of the most important priorities in your life is to find out. If you allow yourself to get in touch with your feelings, you will find that you have very definite, specific preferences. Knowing what you want is a key ingredient in your happiness and joy in life. Love yourself enough to find out what you really want.

Shown below are eight major areas of a balanced life. It is important that you have chosen what you want in each category rather than allowing your family, your culture or another person dictate how it "should" be.

CAREER:	What do you want to achieve in your work?
FAMILY:	What relationships do you want to have?
FINANCIAL:	How much money do you want to have REALLY?
PHYSICAL:	What are your health and fitness goals?
MENTAL:	What do you wish to study and learn more about?
SPIRITUAL:	What are your spiritual goals?
CREATIVITY:	Given no limitations, what would you create?
SOCIAL &	What are your aspirations regarding others?
SERVICE:	How would you like most to serve others?

Exercise for the Eight Areas of Life:

1. List at least 3 things under each of the 8 categories that are most important to you. Choose from your own sense of values. Be sure these are things you really want.

2. For each item on the list, form a clear mental image and use Concentration and Affirmation to program for it.

3. Remember to relax deeply for your Alpha-level Concentration and affirmation process.

4. Feel your feelings - your joy, love, sense of well-being. Feel these feelings emotionally and as body sensations. Hold onto these feelings as long as you can.

5. Allow yourself to feel grateful that your good is now headed toward you in these specific forms.

6. Complete your exercise and return to ordinary waking consciousness.

Create a Time Warp

When you need more time and it seems there is no way to fit everything in — you have only ten minutes until a meeting begins and you are twenty minutes away on the highway — whatever the details of your circumstances, you can create a "time warp."

HOW TO:
Relax and breathe a few deep breaths no matter how tense or agitated you may be feeling. Ask the energy of the Universe to "expand time for me." Visualize arriving at your destination safely and just at the perfect moment. Feel yourself centered and poised and being just on time regardless of clock time. Continue breathing and proceed safely.

Notice that you can do this Concentration without closing your eyes or counting down to the Alpha level. I have used this technique many times while driving in heavy traffic. It is important to relax and breathe and be willing to ask the Universe for help.

I have experienced this technique working very consistently and successfully. Sometimes it has happened that everyone else I was to meet with was also delayed and we all arrived together. At other times heavy traffic would open up and flow much more quickly than could usually be expected. And at other times I have discovered that although my watch reflected that I was late, the clocks in use at my destination were set differently and I was "right on time."

The most important element of this technique is the feeling tone, for it is your feeling that is the most creative element in your life. (Consciousness follows attention and attention follows feelings.) Breathing and allowing the state of relaxed alertness and trust to permeate your body and awareness provides you with peace and calm while you are on the way toward your goal. In our Western culture, we are trained to be so goal oriented that we often neglect to enjoy the journey. The truth is that if the journey is joyful enough, the goal hardly matters. So when you "claim your peace" along the way, you already have succeeded!

Locating Lost Articles

Everything, animate and inanimate, is made of life force energy. When something is lost or misplaced, use the following exercise to locate it again:

Exercise:

Sit or lie down in a comfortable position. Take a few deep breaths and allow your mind to become quiet. Close your eyes and turn your inward gaze toward the mid-spot between the eyebrows. Visualize the missing article there clearly and vividly, then mentally speak to the missing article: "Find me . . .find me."

Feel the peacefulness. Be very still and see if you feel that you have "connected" with the missing article. If so, you need do no more. Simply relax, open your eyes when you wish to and return to ordinary consciousness. Feel relaxed and without time pressure. The article will find you in its own perfect time and way. Forget it for the moment. You have done all you need do.

In some cases when it feels necessary to go on actively looking for something, just continue your search in a relaxed, confident manner, with the feeling that it will "find you." Above all, do not allow a feeling of loss or desperation to take you over because that would actually block the resolution of the problem.

I have experienced after using this method a few times that I can simply pause for a moment wherever I am, close my eyes, make "contact" with the item at the spot between the eyebrows, say "Find me," check to be sure I have made contact, open my eyes and continue whatever I am doing. It usually takes only a few seconds. (Sitting or lying down is no longer necessary.) In the beginning, however, you may achieve better results by stopping your activity to assure you have made the essential "contact" at the inner level.

For Telepathic Communication

This technique can also be used to communicate telepathically with a person. I have used it successfully a number of times to communicate with my daughter when I could not otherwise reach her. Frequently, she has phoned within a few minutes, asking, "Mom, were you looking for me?"

Exercise:

Sit or lie down comfortably. Take a few deep breaths and quiet your mind. Close your eyes and turn your inward gaze upward toward the mid-spot between the eyebrows. Now "see" the person with whom you wish to communicate at that spot and say to him or her, "Call me" (or whatever message you wish to convey). Check to be sure you feel you have made contact with the energy of that person and then just relax and prepare to open your eyes and return to an ordinary waking consciousness level as soon as you wish.

It is important to relax and release the person at the same time that you request them to call you. This allows the message to be received more easily. It is like writing a letter to someone and then mailing it — you have to let it leave your hands in order for it to travel to and be received by the person for whom it is intended. Telepathic energy functions in a similar way; it travels best if you let go.

Drowning Out Negative Chatter

At times all people experience a negative inner voice, chattering away and undermining the quality of life. Whether this negative chatter is a mild irritant or so incessant and loud as to seem maddening, the technique I want to share here will effectively drown that voice out, allowing you to attend to more constructive pursuits.

In Starseed Transmissions, Raphael (through amanuensis Ken Carey) describes a human being as being like a magnificent luminous balloon filled with life force energy which is constantly being replenished from the universal energy field. He adds that guilt and fear are like two giant rips, one in each side of the beautiful membrane, causing the precious life force to pour out and be wasted — a literal hemorrhage of energy. It is, therefore, vitally important to find a specific technique which will serve to stop these massive drains on your life energy. (Read the chapter entitled "Clearing Suppressions: Why and How?") Once you have cleared the bulk of the accumulation of suppressed negative energy, much of the drain will cease. The Drowning Out Technique detailed here, is not intended to serve as a clearing method, but is simply meant to help you at those times when you are occupied in such a way as to make an immediate clearing process inappropriate. At those times, this exercise will minimize or eliminate the effect of those negative messages.

Whether the little ego mind is pulling you out of the present moment with guilt over the past or fear of the future, two sides of the same pernicious coin, you can use the following technique to successfully drown out this destructive chatter.

Drowning Out Technique:

The instant you experience the negative thought, strike right back with an Affirmation you have chosen for this purpose. If the negative voice is loud, retort loudly! If the negative voice is rapid, retort even more rapidly! Repeat your Affirmation as much and for as long and as loud as it takes to effectively drown out the negative inner chatter. If you awake in the middle of the night, for instance, and feel gripped with a feeling of fear over financial insecurity (so common in our culture), you might lie there in the dark and repeat, "I am happy and prosperous!" Then use your willpower to focus on a happy, prosperous scene in your mind as you repeat your Affirmation. The key to remember here is that your consciousness (the creative part) follows your attention. You will have in your life more of whatever you pay attention to. Consequently, you may begin to jealously guard your attentive process in order to create the circumstances you want in your life.

This is one of the techniques which we use at The Firewalk to drown out fearful thoughts. While actually walking across the glowing hot coals, many people use this drowning out technique by repeating "Cool moss.

. . cool moss," and imagining that they are walking across cool moss. And once you have such a powerful experience as this, you will realize that you can use the "Drowning Out Technique" effectively with other kinds of fear.

5

Clearing Suppressions: Why and How?

*In order to experience a different world,
it is necessary not to change the world
but to change you.*

We have been discussing that the mind is the most powerful instrument we have — but most of us are not in contact with the higher mind. And the little conscious mind, functioning alone like a tiny radio out of touch with the transmitting station, is virtually powerless until it reconnects to the source. Signals from the source are blocked by a vast amount of static. That static is comprised of habitual unconscious patterns of behavior, faulty belief systems acquired from family, religion and culture, and suppressions of negative energy, primarily in the form of guilt, regret, anger and fear. Those limited beliefs, biases and prejudices function like filters over the lens of your perception as you view life.

Imagine a clear lens focused out onto a vast panorama. Place over that clear lens a filter with a checkerboard grid pattern; the vast scene can now be viewed only through that overlaying gridwork. Add another filter, this one constructed so that you look through round holes; your perception of the scene beyond will change again; now you will view it only through the smaller openings of the combined checkerboard and round-hole filters. A third filter of grey film will further dull the perceived image. Each successive filter over the lens of your consciousness further constricts and dimishes the light and the view. No matter how beautiful the scene might actually be, it will look pretty much like all the others because you are looking through those same filters. In order to make a change, therefore, it is necessary not to change the scenery, but to begin removing the filters. Then the whole vista will appear as you have never seen it before . . . and what will have changed will all be in your own awareness.

Let us discuss specifically how suppressions function to block your life force energy and cloud the lens through which you look. Suppressed anger, for instance, becomes an energy block precisely because it is stored; if that energy had been felt in the first place (at the time the feeling was stimulated), it would simply have passed through and would have been integrated into the overall awareness of the person. It is the fear or judgment of the anger that is the contaminating factor causing the blockage. This is true of all kinds of suppressed energy. Energy is neither negative nor positive, but when we use the limited understanding of our little conscious minds to label or judge energy, thus deciding whether or not to allow ourselves to feel that energy, then suppression occurs.

These principles are not dependent on the belief of mankind for their operation; Universal principles operate according to Universal law whether anyone believes them or not. Before the invention of the radio, most people did not believe there were such things as radio waves in the surrounding atmosphere, for instance, but the simple radio proved that these sounds were present all along and simply required a proper receiver to "hear them."

In the same fashion, omnipresent in the Universal energy field all around you is abundant knowledge which exists whether or not you are aware of it. When you clear your consciousness sufficiently, suddenly you will "know" things of which you were previously unaware. For instance, you often will perceive another person's suppressed anger, even though he may be hiding it beneath words and body language which would conceal the true feeling. I frequently experience receiving such information in my solar plexus as an uneasiness and I now know to begin paying closer attention in order to discover what is really going on.

This becoming aware of the energy around you, beginning to be sensitive to its information, feels akin to suddenly "waking up." You may wonder how you lived all your life unaware of these powerful energies. You will not be able to receive this information, however, if you have suppressions of negative energy, because your receiving mechanism will be burdened with the static mentioned above. Most people suppress feelings so automatically, having been well trained since early childhood, and have carried those suppressions for so long that they have no sense of what it would be like to be free of them.

It is wonderful to be free of suppressions! It feels powerful, peaceful and happy. You will find that you will not go into reaction with the least provocation, as you may have in the past. Your "buttons" will be pushed far less often. It actually feels like removing those buttons. Something upsetting occurs and you don't feel upset! You would have felt upset before but you don't now. And you can feel your feelings; it isn't that you are out of touch with yourself. You just are not upset by what would have seemed upsetting before!

The human brain is a veritable storehouse of dynamic life force energy, which is constantly utilized to operate the multi-trillion functions of the body and brain. Beyond these automatic functions, each of us is designed to operate as an extension of the Creator but we have forgotten that important fact. We have forgotten our true identity and lost sight of our powerful potential because we are weighted down with suppressions of negative energy. Most of us are wearing a thick shell of limitations which has darkened our awareness for so long we have forgotten it is there. Fear, alone, exhausts an enormous amount of life energy; it is the greatest enemy we have. Fear causes the life force energy, which usually follows a steady flow through the nerves, to be squeezed out; the nerves themselves then become as though paralyzed. The vitality of the entire body and brain becomes depleted.

But what can be done to clear this static? What steps can you take to peel away the barnacles encrusted onto the physical, emotional and psychic bodies? How do you go about changing deep-seated habits which serve only to keep you imprisoned in a powerless way of living? How do you effectively change limiting beliefs that seem so much a part of your heritage you may feel doomed to repeat your family's patterns? How do you rid yourself of anger and fear you usually deny? Suppressions of negative energy may be contaminating your entire life but how can you go about clearing it? It can seem like being caught in a maze without directions for escape.

This is one of the most vitally important subjects of all. When you discover how easy it is to clear this static, you will have embarked on a new level of living. The fastest and most effective way to clear away these blockages is through understanding and using your breathing! You can learn to use your own breathing to clear yourself of all the unwanted, limiting excess baggage.

This may sound too simple to work but remember that it is not necessary to believe or disbelieve anything. A good example of this comes to mind: A gentleman in his sixties phoned me, inquiring about Connected Breathing. He asked many questions, trying to decide if he wanted to make an appointment and finally stated emphatically, "You know, I don't really believe in any of this!" I assured him that belief or non-belief has no bearing, that although sometimes one may cognitively be aware of what is happening in consciousness, that the Connected Breathing/Rebirthing process happens at more of a physical, cellular level outside the mind.

He arrived for his appointment using a cane and wearing a leg brace, the result of polio many years ago. I worked with him for almost two hours during which tears poured down his cheeks while he insisted that he was "feeling nothing!" He had a lot of suppressed rage (he said he was unaware of this) and had alienated just about everyone in his world, from his ex-wife to his grown children. Now he was on the verge of being fired from his job because he was rude to customers (he felt he couldn't help himself!) He left at the end of the session stating repeatedly that he felt "really weird!" (It is not uncommon for a person to experience "calmness" as "really weird" in the beginning. To some people, being calm is a foreign experience!)

The next day he returned for another session and shared the following with me: "For the past six months, my blood pressure has been high and the doctor has tried several different kinds of medication to lower it, all without success, and has yet to find what is causing the high blood pressure in the first place. Today, my blood pressure is normal! My ankles are usually greatly swollen by the end of the day; today they are not swollen at all! And I was able to get through my strenuous day easily." I felt it was clear that the high blood pressure did not respond to medication because it was not physical in the first place! When he got in touch with some of the suppressed anger and released it, like venting a pressure cooker, the pressure became normal.

I have worked with countless men and women who have experienced that their whole life is changed by breathing into suppressed feelings and fully experiencing them. Sometimes physical healings occur; more often the healing is psychological and emotional. A great amount of life force energy is thus freed for positive, creative expression. Healings of body, mind and emotions are common results in many cases.

The material below on Connected Breathing/Rebirthing will serve as an introduction and provide answers to many questions people frequently ask. By allowing yourself the opportunity to have your own experience of it, you then will be able to honestly evaluate it.

6

Connected Breathing/ Rebirthing

"Rebirth is simply the dawning on your mind of what is already in it."   A Course in Miracles

"Offering the inhaling breath into the exhaling breath and offering the exhaling breath into the inhaling breath neutralizes both breaths, releasing prana from the heart and bringing life force under control."
                    Bhagavad-Gita IV:29

Connected breathing, also called rebirthing, is a simple breathing technique, the aim of which is to gently, lovingly clear out mental, emotional and physical blocks and suppressions, especially those arising from birth and early childhood experiences. It is a powerful, simple technique which can transform the quality of your life and all your relationships - with yourself and with others, both loved ones and strangers alike. It can transform your relationship with the physical world as you begin to experience nature, herself, as a living entity; and it can transform your relationship with money and possessions.

The lives of most people are burdened with a great many suppressions and to the extent that this is true is one's life experience blocked. Because these suppressions have been carried for so long, it is common not to realize consciously that they are present. Suppressions of negative energy cause most of the problems in a person's life, ruining potentially good relationships or preventing them altogether. If you have suppressions of guilt or anger, for instance, so widespread in our society, you will experience frequent upset, irritation, frustration and possibly even "accidents". You will tend to find fault with people and situations in the world or you may be constantly finding fault with yourself. You may find yourself taking that anger out on someone you truly love, like your child, when what you really want to experience with that person is joy and fun. A typical reaction when something like that happens is to wonder "what got into me" and resolve to control one's behavior in the future. But this is really like attempting to hold an inflated rubber boat underwater; the minute you relax and stop holding it down, up it pops! When these suppressions are cleared away, those angry reactions just will not be there any more because there will be no energy to fuel them. You will then feel a sense of freedom, energy and wellbeing that may be beyond anything you have experienced!

Heal Yourself With Breathing

In many cases, the very first experience of connected breathing is so powerful and effective that a person feels immediately cleansed and lighter, as though he has had a psychic and emotional bath. It is not uncommon to feel younger and more peaceful than in many years. With the exception of deep meditation, I know of no tool so transformative as connected breathing!

Connected breathing/rebirthing is not a religious practice (though I consider it sacred) nor is it any form of therapy (though it is much faster and more effective than many forms of psychotherapy). It is simply using your breathing to clear and heal yourself of the static which burdens your body, mind and emotions. Underneath it all you are already perfect and when you are clear enough of that static, you will experience that perfection yourself!

What does that mean? Let's explore this a bit. Stating that "you are already perfect..." can sound hollow, like just so much meaningless rhetoric, and your eyes may glaze over as you read the words and miss the meaning altogether. But please read on and I will do my best to describe the experience I am talking about here.

"You are a Spirit which has a body!" Most of us have heard that but what does it mean? Usually it means nothing because it cannot possibly have meaning without an experience! It is as though information goes only an inch deep, while experience penetrates a mile deep into the very core of one's being, bringing about profound and permanent life changes. But we know that so comparatively few people have a meaningful experience. Lots of people read but very few people have a real experience! Then why go on with this paragraph? Because even though life is not an intellectual experience — you cannot "know" life mentally, through information — sometimes having a framework or concept can help you to become open and receptive enough to allow yourself to have an experience. Through connecting the breaths, one is able to gently and naturally let go of suffering, fear, anger, sadness and guilt, which results in a joyful integration of energies. This enhances your capacity to love and to live a happier, more creative and productive life.

The benefits of connected breathing are usually immediate and include:

Stress reduction through deep relaxation
Increased creativity
Better health, more vitality and energy
Emotional stability
Enhanced ability to deal with problems
Increased intelligence
Greater powers of perception
Mental clarity
Greater ability to make positive life changes
Improved, easier personal relationships
Inner peace, compassion, lasting happiness
Sense of well-being
Enlightenment and expanding awareness
Experience of being centered, poised, connected
A deep sense of life purpose and meaning.

It helps to be aware that it is not the addition of something from outside that gives joy and the bliss of higher consciousness. It is the power of your inner receptivity that determines how much and how quickly you can attune to the higher vibrations. By clearing the channels of your inner receptivity, you can quicken your upward evolutionary process. You will discover that you have nothing to attain; you already are perfect . . . a child of God! The whole process, then, is a matter of becoming consciously aware of who you are - of realizing the true identity of the Self. Connected breathing/rebirthing with a qualified, caring professional Rebirther is one of the fastest ways to clear the inner channels, opening the way for the ever-present Light and love to pour through!

Below, I have given information which is practical to know before actually experiencing a rebirthing session. While it is true that you must experience connected breathing to really know what it is, I find that having some conceptual understanding can assist you in surrendering more easily to the process.

Breath is the Missing Link!

The missing link between spirit (soul) and matter (body) is the breath; specifically, this element in the breath is life force energy. In India it is called prana and in Japan it is referred to as "ki," as in the Japanese discipline of Aikido. Breathing begins at birth and ceases at death. Humans can live for weeks without food, for days without water but only about three minutes without breathing. Knowing that this life force energy is the secret to human evolution, the ancient sages of India have long taught the science of the breath. Let's take a closer look at breathing and how and why it is so powerfully interwoven into our life experience.

A Child's First Breath

When a child is born, his first breath is usually taken simultaneously with feelings of fear, cold, separation (from mother), loud noises, bright lights, and being handled by strangers. The baby has spent its entire existence in the protective environment of mother's womb, in a perfect temperature of 100 degrees. Now suddenly he has been bombarded by great contractions forcing him out into a world which seems frightening indeed. Just as you may associate feelings and past experiences with a certain music or smell, as a baby you may have associated many negative feelings with breathing.

69

Because of the association at birth between breathing and negative feelings, we usually hold our breath to some extent whenever we are experiencing stress of any kind. This is an unconscious mechanism for avoiding the pain we experienced along with that first breath. Subsequently, we ordinarily breathe in an unobstructed manner only when we are relaxed and feeling calm and safe.

A key factor in the suppression (storage) of negative energy into the subconscious mind is this: when you hold your breath, any experience that is occurring in your mind, emotions or body will store.*

Connecting the Breaths Releases Suppressions

The way to empty the subconscious mind of suppressions is to fully feel them while breathing. When a suppression is coming up out of the subconscious mind and becoming conscious, a person will often experience it just as he would have had he felt it originally. (If fear was suppressed, he will feel afraid; if anger was suppressed, he will feel angry.) But the energy that is suppressed was not experienced at the time the stress occurred, usually because it did not feel safe to feel it. The fear or judgment of the feeling is what caused it to store in the first place. And, stored in the subconscious mind, it carries a high charge of energy and is very powerful; as a matter of fact, it is this stored

---

*It is interesting to note that the technology called Superlearning utilizes the holding of the breath in a desirable way. (Superlearning is a method wherein learning occurs much more rapidly than usual and with phenomenal retention even long afterward.) The material being presented by the Superlearning teacher is "input" during a rhythmic breathing cycle while the student is holding his breath. Apparently some mechanism built into our human neurology causes experience to store when the breath is held.

energy that attracts events into a person's life. For instance, if you are repressing anger, the unconscious energy of that stored anger will attract some person or situation into your life to get you in touch with that anger. So you will actually be "placing an order" for something to come along to upset or anger you. This is how your Higher Self works to get you to cleanse the inside. Once you have emptied the suppressed anger, there will be far fewer experiences in your life to feel angry about.

Unless you clear yourself and achieve alignment of your unconscious mind with your conscious mind, it will be the unconscious part that will determine what goes on in your life. Desiring to consciously choose your life experience instead of being governed by unconscious forces is reason enough to pursue the connected breathing process, even if there were no other benefits.

When a person begins connected breathing, those suppressions will begin to loosen and move up into consciousness. This explains the frequently-reported experiences people have in breathing sessions. Rather than a memory, it is much more like actually experiencing a stored event. It is common to re-experience your birth, including details like who was present at the birth, the feelings they had, whether or not you were separated from mother, whether she nursed you, etc.

Are You Uncomfortable Around Children?

If, as a child, you suffered hurts, limitations, misunderstandings or abuses which you have not yet forgiven and, therefore, your little inner child self is still very wounded, you may feel angry and judgmental when you are around children or young people. I observe this happening especially if that child or young person has been treated well and allowed freedom to develop him/herself with unconditional love and tolerance. Being around that child will often make an adult aware of his sadness over his own wounded inner child self, and he will often react with anger and judgment: "That child should be taught to respect his elders!" (The real feeling underneath that statement is often, "I wasn't treated well when I was a child and when I now see a child who is treated well, I feel so sad because I become aware again of what I missed and of the pain I felt as a child!" You may be horrified to admit even to yourself that you actually feel this way!) I am not suggesting that childish misbehavior be condoned. What I am suggesting is that you observe yourself and your reactions, and if you find yourself in a state of angry reaction over the conduct of a child, you may want to begin some self-examination and consider beginning a healing process for your own wounded inner child self.

Children often act out the unconscious energy of a person or group of people — they mirror for us what is *really* happening in energy — and it may be that the child is behaving the way he is unconsciously as a way to help you to get in touch with something deep inside you that needs to be forgiven and healed! Please do not ignore these theories without checking into it honestly within yourself. It can provide a very wonderful healing opportunity for you.

You will know that you have achieved a lot of healing for your inner child self when you can be in the presence of a child who misbehaves and simply, calmly and lovingly take any corrective action which is appropriate, if any, *without becoming angry or out of control yourself!* (In other words, you won't get "hooked" by the energy because there is no suppressed anger inside you to get hooked. Remember that when an orange is squeezed, orange juice comes squirting out because that's what was inside in the first place. Whatever comes out of you when you are squeezed is what was already inside you!)

Breathe to Clear Your Consciousness

The breath could be compared to pumping clear water into the end of a hose which has a clog in it. If the water continues, the clog will be partially or wholly loosened and moved out to clear the conduit entirely. About ten breathing sessions are usually recommended to clear most of the accumulation of suppressed negative energy. At that point, most people are adept enough at understanding the process of connected breathing to clear themselves and/or to trade breathing sessions with a "buddy."

Choosing a Rebirther

In selecting a rebirther, it is very important to feel safe, comfortable and trusting of him or her. If you have any discomfort, be willing to immediately communicate about that discomfort. You may want to determine the nature and extent of his or her training, how s/he feels about his/her clients, how s/he knows when a breathing session is over, and whether or not s/he loves his/her work! (If the primary reason for choosing this profession is other than sheer love for it, find another rebirther!)

There are some organizations which certify trainees, however, certification, alone, or lack of it, is not a sufficient criterion. While breathing skills are important, even more important is the personal and spiritual integrity of the rebirther. He or she should be clear and have clear relationships with self and with others. His integrity should be beyond question and he should be mature enough to put his own concerns aside during the time he is working with a client.

A rebirther must be truly competent in many ways. It is good to remember that spirituality is ultimate balance and that it gives rise to the keenest intelligence. There should be a balance in all areas of his life and common sense will prevail. A sincere, dedicated Rebirther is one who has cleared most of his or her own suppressions and who places the highest value on his own spiritual attunement. This will include a healthy balance in all areas: physical, psychological, emotional, personal, professional, all areas of relationship and service. A good Rebirther knows that all the answers you need will come through your own awareness and, therefore, will aim toward helping you tune into your inner space. He or she will support you to hear from within yourself the direction that is most appropriate for you in any area of your life, with no judgment about what you "should" do.

While it is true that connected breathing, alone, will serve to help you feel and integrate suppressions, the physical presence of the rebirther is vitally important in the beginning. A good rebirther will be able to see beyond the "appearances" around you to what is really going on at the energy level in your life. A rebirther who is connected to his own Higher Self and, therefore, knows his own true identity, can see your true identity, too. Holding the vision of that awareness for you while you go through the releasing and integration of negative suppressions, can help you to expand into a higher level of expression when you are ready. If this does not make much sense now, know that it will make utter sense after you have had the experience of connecting with the expanded consciousness. Attempting to describe what this expanded experience is like without having had the experience itself could be compared to trying to describe the taste of an exotic fruit you had never seen or tasted. All the descriptions would mean very little, and just one taste would communicate all that is necessary.

Before every breathing session, I center myself and make sure I am connected with the Light of my Higher Self, asking the Holy Spirit to take charge of the entire session. In addition I appeal to the Higher Self of the person or persons who are going to rebirth, asking illumination, help and healing for the individual(s). I then formally dedicate the rebirth session with this prayer:

> "Heavenly Father-Mother God: We commit and
> release this experience to the healing power of the
> Holy Spirit for the highest good. So be it and so it is!"

The Holy Spirit utilizes the body, mind, energy and consciousness of the rebirther in much the same way a crystal is used in a radio or TV to augment the energy which is available for that purpose. Many of my rebirthing clients have incredibly blissful, enlightening experiences and I am the first to acknowledge that I, consciously, do not know how to achieve any such thing for them. This is a constant reminder to me that it is not I doing the work, but the Holy Spirit working through me. I believe that the Holy Spirit is so abundant and omnipresent that it will flow through any channel which is open enough. The channel is not important, of itself. Rather, the important consideration is whether or not it is relatively free of obstacles to the Light.

Sex, Drugs and Rebirthing

A connected breathing session is very intimate in that the Rebirther is usually very closely aligned, psychically and emotionally, with his client. He or she may feel the same feelings and even see the same images that the breather is experiencing inwardly. But it is entirely inappropriate to combine sex or sexual touching and connected breathing!

Your rebirther may touch you appropriately by wiping tears from your eyes, holding your hand, touching your arm, touching your forehead or hair, etc., all as gestures of support and love. However, any touching that is sexual in nature is completely out of line. Even when a person serves as a rebirther for his or her own spouse, the connected breathing experience should be clearly separated from the space of their lovemaking.

A good rebirther will honor the space of your being with respect and reverence for all aspects of you and herself. Trust the intelligence of your body and your inner guidance to direct you in the choice of a rebirther. As in most professions, there are a few who may lack integrity; it is up to you to listen to your still, small, inner voice when you select a rebirther. And if you begin with one person and do not feel comfortable, give yourself permission to find another professional with whom you are comfortable. Read the section entitled, "Trusting Your Body." It will help you in this and many other life decisions.

Illegal drugs have no appropriate place in a healthy life and they certainly have no place in rebirthing. While drugs may alter your awareness and make you think you are having a spiritual experience, you will discover that it is not the real thing. Connected breathing is a way to get in touch with your life force energy; drugs are a way to shut down your life force energy. They serve as a distraction to your becoming more alive, delaying your discovery of your real nature as a divine being!

In addition, if you are taking a prescription medication which functions to alter your moods, such as an anti-depressant, a tranquilizer of any kind, etc., it is usually appropriate to stop the drug, give yourself and your body time to clear the drug and then begin rebirthing. I usually decline to rebirth a person who is taking any mood-altering drug because it would be counterproductive. Mood-altering drugs block your feelings; as stated before, connected breathing puts you in touch with your feelings and integrates them! On occasion there are exceptions to this, such as when the medication is administered to counteract a depression which is primarily physically based. Feel free to discuss any of these issues with your rebirther to clarify any questions you have.

All addiction is illness. It is a clear signal that a person is out of balance if he is taking illegal drugs or prescription drugs for the purpose of altering his moods or awareness. This includes rebirthers. My recommendation is that you avoid connected breathing with any rebirther who is using drugs from the above categories.

I have rebirthed a number of people who are in recovery after active alcohol or drug addiction. One man had been actively addicted to alcohol and a whole range of drugs, including cocaine, and had been in recovery for about 2 years when I began guiding him through breathing sessions. After several sessions of connected breathing and appropriate classes, he began experiencing a much greater sense of self-esteem and well-being, and a lot of joy and love for himself and everyone else. He phoned me one day in the middle of his busy work schedule and shared the following, which I feel is so encouraging for anyone, especially those who are or have been addicted: "I feel so happy that I can't stop smiling," he giggled. "I was in the lobby of an office building and saw an older lady in a wheelchair, a complete stranger, and I felt so much love for her! I have never before even imagined that a feeling like this existed. If addicts knew about this experience, no one would ever take drugs! There is no drug high that can compare to this!"

It is usually a good idea to be in recovery for at least 6 months prior to beginning a connected breathing program. For active addiction, Alcoholics Anonymous and Narcotics Anonymous provide a wonderful service. Connected breathing does not replace or substitute for these fine organizations with their excellent programs and dedicated people. Be where you are and receive all the healing you can along the way. When it is time to begin rebirthing, you will continue to heal in a balanced way, building on a strong foundation of recovery.

Co-Dependency/Adult Children of Alcoholics

Because the issues of co-dependency affect a majority of people today, it is helpful to understand more about them. You may wish to inquire into groups which sponsor excellent meetings all over the country. Many families are dysfunctional even without the presence of alcohol or drugs. Co-dependency issues involve many false, limiting beliefs, which can be healed. Becoming more conscious and aware can only support your continued growth and development and thus your happiness! Rebirthing is sometimes a very helpful tool to add to your recovery process if you have co-dependency issues to work through. It can be a wonderful assurance of love and safety to help you through some frightening zones of seeing more clearly the life you lived while growing up. The rebirthing experience can help speed you through the pain of becoming more aware and begin the process of forgiveness sooner.

People who are of sound mental health and who truly desire to grow and be even more healthy and happy can greatly benefit by rebirthing. It is a tool not just for coping, but for true healing. Rebirthing is not meant to take the place of therapies of any kind intended for those requiring such treatment. However, it often can support other forms of treatment at the appropriate time. My rebirthing practice has included clients who are psychologists, ministers, chiropractors and physicians. In addition these professionals refer their patients to me when they believe that the connected breathing process can support and augment the patient's healing.

Quite obviously, if you are not ready to begin making changes in your life, you are not ready for connected breathing. It is important to follow your own feelings and not allow anyone else to impose a "should" on you. While it is wonderful to open up and grow when one is truly ready, it is also okay to be content with your life just as it is and take longer with your evolutionary process. If it is okay with you, it is okay, period! But if you experience difficulties with relationships which resist your efforts to resolve them, if your finances persist at a less-than-acceptable level for you to live a healthy, balanced, satisfying life, if you feel driven in any area of life, then you may find healing through rebirthing.

There is a listing at the back of this book for locating psychologists, rebirthers and other caring, conscious professionals and organizations in various parts of the world who are available to supply assistance or information. No licensing or certification process, however, can guarantee the integrity of an individual or substitute for your own inner knowingness. Whenever you are seeking the services of a professional, whether a lawyer, a doctor, a psychologist or a rebirther, it is advisable to select wisely. As mentioned so often in these pages, it is important to feel peaceful and comfortable in your choice and is never appropriate to abdicate your personal power to any other person or organization. Honor yourself by being true to your own common sense and inner guidance.

Accepting Your Feelings

It is important to have a balanced perspective toward suppressions. The energies which we are used to calling "negative," are just feelings. They really are neither negative nor positive; they just are. But many people do not have permission from family, culture, religion and thus not from themselves, to feel negative feelings, especially anger. Judging these feelings in the first place is what caused them to become suppressed; if they had been perceived as acceptable, they would have been experienced at the time of the stress. So it is critical now, to accept and feel them in order to clear yourself.

The suppressions which are dislodged and experienced with breathing are not "released" but actually are integrated into the totality of your expanded awareness. Think about the following example: Most likely, you have had some experience in your life that was quite painful but, because of that experience, you matured and became more compassionate, sensitive, and understanding. In other words you *expanded* because of integrating that pain into your total awareness. That is exactly what happens with rebirthing. The energy of a negative, painful event which you did not feel in the moment it occurred, became stored, instead, in your subconscious mind as suppressed energy. When you breathe and allow yourself to fully feel that suppressed energy, it is brought up into consciousness and integrated in just the same way, leaving you more mature and expanded! People frequently experience after rebirthing that "even the trees look different." It is as though some filter is removed which had partially obstructed the lens through which they viewed the world and, indeed, the world now looks different, usually simpler, lighter and happier.

Compare the breath to a train moving across country with you as a passenger. Let us say that as long as you are breathing in a connected fashion during a rebirth, the train continues moving. If you stop breathing, the train stops. Now suppose that you come to a particularly unpleasant place where the scenery is unpleasant and it evens smells bad! You can keep the train moving and even speed it up or you can stop the train and take a long look at this unsightly place. Compare that to reaching a space in a breathing session where perhaps you are in touch with some energy that is particularly painful. If you hold your breath, it is tantamount to stopping the train so you can experience it for a longer time. So it makes more sense to keep breathing and even speed up the breath to move through this space quickly.

The Connected Breath

Now I will describe the actual rebirthing or connected breath. Let us use mouth breathing as an example. Open the mouth rather wide and draw in with intention and willpower on the inhalation; then immediately exhale, just allowing the breath to fall away. You will not "follow the breath out" or blow out or control the exhalation or try to make it the same duration as the inhalation. Just let go and allow it to fall away as if you were dropping a ball off a cliff. This is a vital point. Many people will attempt to control the outbreath in some way, as they probably attempt to control their own lives. If the exhale is controlled IN ANY WAY, it is not a rebirthing breath!

Next point: No pauses before or after you inhale or exhale. This is another way some people unconsciously attempt to control the process. Initially, you may have many random thoughts and all are okay. You may feel that you are taking too much time, that you don't know how to do it right, that this isn't going to work, that you are hungry, thirsty, wish this were over, feel really weird, wonder if you've gone crazy, feel like your throat is too dry, etc. And none of those thoughts matter at all because this process happens outside of the mind. Sometimes the mind is involved, but it is not required to cooperate in the rebirthing process, which is why the breath is so powerful.

Three Ways to Breathe

1. **Fast and full** - used in the beginning of a rebirth to really pump a lot of energy into the body. I usually have a client begin with wide-open mouth breathing, although it is okay to breathe in and out through the nose also. One may also begin with mouth breathing,

then switch to nose breathing for a while and even back to mouth breathing again later on. It is not acceptable to breathe in through the mouth and out through the nose or vice versa.

2. **Fast and shallow** - this is like speeding up the film through a movie projector (faster speed) and turning down the volume or intensity of the feeling (shallow depth). It is not necessary to be overwhelmed by an experience in order to fully experience and thus integrate it into your conscious awareness. You may love your favorite music but you probably would not choose to have it playing so loud it would hurt your ears!

3. **Slow and full** - This mode is utilized when you are experiencing something that you want to fully enjoy or absorb. It is sometimes used at the end of a breathing session if you get into a very joyful, loving space and want to feel every last bit of the feeling.

Hyperventilation

The Random House Dictionary defines hyperventilation as "excessively rapid and deep breathing resulting especially in the decrease of carbon dioxide in the blood." This phenomenon can only occur when the breathing is inhibited, therefore, there is no reason to fear it in rebirthing. Specifically, hyperventilation is caused by controlling the exhalation by blowing or forcing the breath out in some way, or attempting to make the exhaling breath the same duration as the inhaling breath.

The correct connected breath is simply allowed to "fall away" with no control of any kind on your part. This point is very important! People who are afraid of their own feelings and/or their own thoughts sometimes attempt to control the exhalation in some way. They may "push" on the breath, as if they want to get rid of something bad. Notice that this is "making something wrong" and the way around it is to "let everything be okay . . . now."

Fear and resistance to relaxation and breathing can tend to create symptoms of tetany and hyperventilation. The more relaxed you are with the connected breathing process, the less likely you are to be inconvenienced by any of these symptoms. An easy way to treat symptoms of breathlessness, dizziness or feelings of panic, should they arise on any occasion, is simply to breathe into a paper bag or into your cupped hands. This will normalize the balance of carbon dioxide and oxygen and symptoms will disappear.

The breath is often an indicator of how you live your life. If you control your breath, you are most likely controlling your life somehow. And right now you may be responding, "Well, of course, I am controlling my life! What else?" The good news is that it is unnecessary to control your life!

Imagine the pilot of a jet airliner. Think about the complexity of the equipment in the cockpit, the enormity of the aircraft itself and the responsibility for a planeload of passengers. Is the pilot *controlling* this airplane or is he *in control* of it? Of course, he is *in control* of it. In this example, it is immediately obvious that the plane is too big and its mechanism much too complex to even think of *controlling* it! A good pilot will trust the cockpit instruments to give him information which will enable him to respond appropriately to all the vital factors involved in safe flying. He is trained to take into account the information supplied by the instruments and adjust his actions accordingly. He relies on his ability to respond intelligently. He can thus carry out his very vital role in a relaxed and confident manner. He is in control.

Are You Controlling or in Control?

This is a very important distinction! Whether you are controlling or in control of your life will make a very major difference in the quality of your health, your business affairs and all your relationships. If you have a thought that you must control your life or anything in it, then you are working very hard. And there is no reason to attempt to control anything! Think about that for a moment. Can you control anything? Do you have the power to control that your heart will be beating even two minutes from now? Of course not! But if you have not examined this subject, you may have a thought that you must control things.

As you begin to trust your unconscious self more, you will be able to begin surrendering, willing to do your best and give it to God. It's okay to be "in control," meaning centered, poised, balanced and using your intelligence to achieve optimum results. "Controlling" is when you have a thought that you have to do it by yourself or that you have to *make* something happen or not happen. Control is a form of fear and is the opposite of love. If you have any doubt of this, just look around in your life and locate a person who is very controlling and see if you feel loved thereby. People turn to controlling instead of trusting life; somewhere along the line such people have made a decision that they are unsafe unless they control everything. Although that decision may have been forgotten, it is running the life of that person and demeaning the quality of his or her life experience.

If you honestly investigate this, you will realize that

it is not possible to control anything. Just shifting the way you think about this will help you to relax and become more effectively in control.

Everything is Already Perfect!

There is a vast and orderly intelligence at work in the Universe; it is functioning perfectly whether you are aware of it or not. If it does not seem to be functioning perfectly in your life, the chances are that you are controlling something — which is a way to keep the perfection away. You are, then, literally holding the perfection out! While it works to have a preference for a certain outcome, being "attached" to or insisting on having only a certain outcome is the way to disadvantage yourself. Allow these concepts enough room to notice how they are working in your life!

Tetany

The term "tetany" is generally used to refer to the state of muscular contractions which sometimes occurs during a breathing session. It usually involves the mouth and hands, but can be anywhere in the body. While it may be experienced as being uncomfortable at the moment, there is nothing dangerous or permanent about tetany during rebirthing. Most people who have done connected breathing have experienced some tetany, usually in the initial sessions.

When tetany occurs in rebirthing, it is appropriate to totally relax and surrender to your breath as you exhale, just allowing it to "fall away." Controlling the outbreath in any way can cause tetany. The following may be helpful for you to know regarding tetany:

1. There is nothing to resist. If it becomes intense and your attention is drawn to it, focus on the sensation you feel in your body and let it be okay; don't make

it wrong. All energy is divine. If the divine energy is more intense in one part of your body than is comfortable, you can choose to welcome it in, appreciate it, then invite it lovingly to disperse throughout your body instead of being so concentrated in one place.

2. Controlling the outbreath often is a signal that you are controlling somewhere in your life. So tetany can be very supportive feedback that you are too much into "doingness" and not enough into "beingness."

3. Breathe fast and shallow to help the tension rapidly integrate into your entire body and awareness. If you have had any experience with the LaMaze breathing which is used in natural childbirth, you will recognize a similarity here. During the intense contractions of labor, the mother is trained to breathe in a fast, shallow manner which is closely akin to this mode of the rebirthing breath. The metaphor here is similar, too, for a laboring mother breathes and stays present, knowing that she is surrendering to the process of new life being born through her. In connected breathing, you are doing the very same thing — you are allowing the birth process for your new life to occur!

Just a word about crying during a breathing session. Crying, of course, often accompanies feelings of sadness, however, we often stop breathing fully when we cry, and simultaneously close up the throat. More recommended as a way to cry during rebirthing is to allow the tears to just flow out of your eyes while you keep connecting your breaths.

About Drama . . .

Connected breathing is a rapid, effective way to bring up and integrate suppressions. This is usually best done in a quiet, quick, efficient manner. Moaning, groaning or sobbing are okay if they are really natural expressions, but it is possible to actually be distracted by your own drama in such cases. It can be the repetition of old habits you have unconsciously held over from infancy and early childhood when you learned to dramatize your way of expression to be sure to get mother's attention. ("Mother won't come to take care of me unless I cry really loud and make it sound like I am in a lot of pain.") The trouble is that when you make a decision like that as a baby, and begin expressing yourself accordingly, you then forget that you decided to do that in the first place (it goes unconscious). If there is a possibility that you may have some of this behavior pattern, it can be very healing for you to do the following:

1. Own it. Tell the truth about it, at least to yourself! (i.e., "I'm not really hurting as bad as it seems but I'm afraid I won't get my needs met unless I make a lot of racket!")

2. Be willing to let it go. It's not part of you; it's holding you back. If you become defensive about this, you can be pretty sure you are playing some game here. When you have let go of all these artificial aspects, you will be left with the glorious gift of your own self-realization! I encourage you to hurry toward your own healing!

3. Trust your rebirther and the feedback you receive from him or her. If you have chosen well, this person can serve you in a magnificent, loving way.

Water Rebirthing

After you have had enough experience with connected breathing to feel truly relaxed and confident with the process, you will welcome the opportunity to breathe through any suppressions that may become conscious. At this point your rebirther will probably suggest rebirthing in warm water. Usually done in a hot tub or swimming pool in water about 100 degrees, warm water rebirthing simulates the experience of being in the womb and the birth process. It is very common to re-experience your birth.

Water rebirthing is more intense than dry rebirthing and, therefore, it is important for you to be skilled at breathing into the extra energy that may move through your body in a way relaxed enough to allow it to integrate into your overall awareness. The exception to this is when a person is not in touch with either his body feelings or psychic awareness, in which case the breath coach may rebirth him in warm water as a way to activate the energy of his feelings.

Cold water rebirthing is sometimes even more intense than in warm water. It can call up feelings of intense fear relating to birth trauma — in most cases the birthing room is much colder than the 100-degree temperature of the womb. Sometimes that cold is associated with the pain of separation from mother and the whole birth process. In addition, it can bring up fears of dying. In case you are wondering why in the world you would want to bring up fears of dying, just consider the following: Would you rather have those fears suppressed in your unconscious or bring them up into consciousness where they can be integrated and thus de-energized? Unless you have dealt with your fears of dying, they are suppressed in your unconscious mind!

Connected Breathing is a very effective and powerful tool for clearing your consciousness and keeping it clear. Using it along with Affirmation, Concentration, and Meditation is even more effective.

7

Meditation

*"Mankind is engaged in an eternal quest for that
'something else' he hopes will bring him happiness,
complete and unending. For those individual souls
who have sought and found God, the search is over:
He is that 'something else.'"*

Paramahansa Yogananda

Meditation is concentration which helps you to become aware of your true self, not the little separate sense of self, but your real self. It helps you to come home to your heart, to come home to your God Self. *

Meditation reconnects you with the source of power within you, cleansing your mind and leaving you open and receptive to creative ideas, solutions to problems, intuition and inspiration. It will alert you when you have gone wide of your mark and guide you to your right road again. You tap into the awareness of being one with everyone and everything in the Universe because, as you meditate, you blend into the energy of Universal Mind. Your nervous system gets a complete rest, more

*The word "meditation" (like the word "guru") has been greatly distorted and overused by the media. There seems to be confusion about what actually constitutes "meditation." At the beginning of a recent class, one participant described her meditation practice as "listening to a subliminal tape as I fall asleep." Another person thought that "just relaxing and not thinking of anything in particular" was the same as meditating.   Still another responded that "almost anything can be thought of as meditation as long as it makes you feel calm." While these activities may be enjoyable and beneficial in your life, it is helpful to realize that they are not meditation! Scientific meditation, properly done, "works like mathematics" and you can be assured of reliable results in your life.

so than it does when you sleep, yet you remain awake and alert. Stress is discharged and your entire being is recharged and refreshed. Just as a musician practices his instrument, when you meditate, your mind is being tuned and trained to operate at its highest potential.

Through the regular practice of meditation, you will actually become more of a genius because you are accessing information and power beyond the scope of your limited conscious mind and allowing it to flow through you. Recalling that one definition of the word "genius" is "guardian spirit," you will discover that, indeed, with just a little practice of meditation, you will become aware that a loving, intelligent presence is guiding and watching over you.

There are so many benefits of meditation that it is no wonder the practice is growing by leaps and bounds in the Western culture! There are no negative side effects and you will experience that every area of your life is greatly enriched, from your business to personal, spiritual, social and family life. Below I have mentioned just a few benefits from the practice of meditation:

Meditation Has Many Benefits

1. Better physical health. Medical authorities today agree that unless stress is alleviated, no program of nutrition or exercise will work to maintain health. Meditation is the most effective way to relieve stress. Dr. Bernie Siegel, a surgeon who recently wrote "Love, Medicine and Miracles", expresses faith that people can participate in their own cures by what he calls "self-induced healing." In his book, Dr. Siegel documents numerous case histories which indicate that by choosing to adopt a new attitude and allow more love and peacefulness into their lives, even patients who have been considered terminally ill have been able to heal themselves through the practice of regular meditation, particularly when accompanied by visualization. Imagine how much

improved one's health becomes when he begins meditation with a strong body!

2. Addictions, including strong drug addictions, have been cured when all other methods have failed. One person who was in recovery after being addicted to drugs continuously for over 15 years began going through connected breathing sessions with me, and he also began to meditate every day. After just a few weeks, he phoned me to share that he was feeling more peace, health and well-being than he could ever remember, adding that "if addicts knew this experience was possible, no one would ever take drugs!"

3. All the body systems rest and become recharged, the heart and lungs and nervous systems.

4. As stress is relieved, a state of relaxed alertness is attained which lasts beyond the period of meditation itself, bringing about expanded creative and mental ability. Scores on IQ tests increase after a person becomes a regular meditator, indicating that the intuitive or metaphoric right side of the brain is being called into opertion with the left brain in a more balanced way.

5. Memory becomes sharper.

6. Meditators generally get along better with others in personal relationships, in business or in the marketplace.

7. Self-image is greatly enhanced with just a little meditation.

8. Those who meditate experience less depression and generally feel capable of meeting any stressful challenge with a sense of personal connectedness and power.

9. People who meditate use less alcohol, drugs and tobacco.

10. Meditators watch much less television, which is often a very potent, negative form of mental programming, freeing up valuable hours for satisfying, productive activities.

The Goal is Reunion with Self

If you begin meditating solely to reap one or more of these benefits, you will accomplish that. Many people begin to meditate, initially, to relieve stress and are pleased to discover that it leads them to much more expansion in consciousness than they anticipated. It is helpful to remember, however, that the true purpose of meditation is not all these benefits but to re-establish contact with your Higher Self, which is the real source of your power. If you approach a meditation practice with that in mind you will reap the greatest benefit. The greatest awakening you can experience is the realization of your own potential. Any achievement is possible when you properly unite will, intelligence, conscience and right action.

Meditation: When?

Meditate first thing in the morning before breakfast to align yourself for the day. With the stomach empty and the digestive system at rest, you will have a great deal of energy with which to focus on your priorities and help you to be receptive to guidance for the day.

Another meditation period at the end of your day and before your evening meal can help you relax and let go of any stress accumulated during the day. If you can arrange additional periods of meditation throughout the day and just before bedtime, you will find it is easy to remain poised all the time.

I like to meditate for a few minutes every hour throughout the day when I can possibly do so and I find that this simple practice added to my regular meditation periods creates a powerful focus for my attention. It also allows me to extend my productive hours longer than normally comfortable.

Where?

Set aside one location for meditation, for you will be creating a strong vibration of peace in that place. It can be a whole room or a corner of a room which is arranged neatly and simply. After a while you will discover that just sitting in that area will be a calming experience. While it is good to have such a place, do not allow yourself to become attached to the accoutrements themselves. It is the inner experience that is truly valuable and you can have that anywhere and anytime you sit in the silence and practice your technique! Meditate outdoors or near a body of water sometimes and be open to the additional life force energy abundant in nature!

How Long?

A meditation period of at least fifteen or twenty minutes will begin to bring noticeable positive results in your life. It is usually better to begin with shorter meditations and gradually extend to longer ones. It is not appropriate to "compete" in your meditation; you are not in a contest with yourself or anyone else. Allow your inner guidance to lead you step by step along your journey.

Preparing for Meditation

It is very helpful to bathe or shower before your meditation (yes, twice a day!). Comfortably warm water balances the nervous system and washes away any unsettling vibrations you may have acquired. While in the water, breathe in and out, connecting your breaths (connecting the inhale and exhale), allowing yourself to feel any feelings that come into your awareness. Remember that feelings are not good or bad — they just are — and it is safe for you to feel them now.

After your bath, dress in clean clothing; clothing carries vibrations and you will be most comfortable if you wear the cleanest clothes possible.

Tense and relax your whole body several times, expelling all the breath suddenly when you exhale, and simultaneously relax completely. Feel that you go limp like a rag doll after exhaling.

Use Correct Meditation Posture

Sit slightly forward on a straight chair with both feet flat on the floor. Your back will not touch the chair. Tilt the body just slightly forward to be sure there is no pressure on the tailbone. Turn your palms upward and place the backs of your hands at the junctions of your hips and thighs, which will keep your shoulders back. Hold your head high, stretching upwards, chin level with the floor. It may help to imagine that there is an imaginary string attached to the very top of your head. If this feels unfamiliar initially, just stay with it. It will become very comfortable as you proceed in meditation.

Life force energy flows up and down along the spinal column to the brain and back downward again. This vital life force is the very energy of aliveness. By maintaining the proper posture, you allow this life force energy to flow unimpeded, healing and recharging your entire mind and body at a deep, cellular level.

You are now ready to practice the meditation given below, a simple but powerful technique, or any other technique you have chosen.

Meditation

Sit with spine erect and feet flat on the floor. Close your eyes and turn your inward gaze to the mid-spot between your eyebrows. This is the location of an energy center which is called the Christ Center, the Ajna Chakra, the Kutastha Chaitanya — it has many names. Just allow your thoughts to go by as though you are watching driftwood float down a stream — no need to grab hold of any piece of it — just let it go by.

Focus your attention on your breath. Become aware of your breathing. When you breathe in, be aware that you are breathing in. When you breathe out, be aware that you are breathing out. At the same time, internally, silently verbalize, "Now I am breathing in. Now I am breathing out." Keep this up for about 5 minutes.

Now become aware of the touch of the air as it enters your nostrils . . . and the touch of the air as it leaves your nostrils. Do not focus your attention on the air as it goes into and out of your lungs; just keep your attention at the nostrils. Where do you feel the touch of the air when you inhale? Where, exactly, do you feel it when you exhale? Do not change the rhythm of your breathing and do not attempt to deepen it. Just let it be the way it is. And observe it.

If you become distracted, that's okay. You may observe your distraction for awhile. If you become bored, be aware of your boredom. In what part of your body do you experience it? It has some repercussion in your body. Having found that out, return to the awareness, to the touch of the air in your nostrils as it goes in and out. Do not strain. Continue this for at least 2 or 3 more minutes. Then gently open your eyes. Retain the feeling of peacefulness as long as possible after your meditation.

You can expand your experience and graduallly enlarge your consciousness by practicing for longer and longer periods. This meditation is simple to do but profound in its effects. The breath is the link between spirit (soul) and matter (physical body). The fastest way to change your consciousness is to change your breathing. This meditation will yield positive results and is safe for anyone to use.

All Paths Lead to God

After several years of searching for my own meditation discipline, I found Kriya Yoga, a connected breath technique which greatly speeds up spiritual evolution. Kriya Yoga is taught by authorized ministers of Self-Realization Fellowship. If you are interested in learning more about Kriya Yoga, you may contact Self-Realization Fellowship directly. The address is included in the list at the back of this book.

There is no one path of meditation that is right for everyone — all paths lead to God. So the important thing is that you seek until you find a path that truly satisfies your own heart — which only you can know — and then commit yourself to that path. Just as you will arrive at your destination faster by choosing one highway and staying on it instead of switching from this road to that, you will make faster progress if you stay with one meditation discipline.

When various paths ascend a mountain, they are, necessarily, widely separated at the beginning, near the broad base of the mountain. However, the higher you travel, the closer together the paths become, so that eventually all the paths converge as they reach the summit. This is an apt metaphor for what we are witnessing at this time on our planet: we are seeing the paths converge as scientists discover what spiritual masters have long stated — that mind is the creator of what we call material reality. As our world shrinks, becoming a "global village," it is becoming easier to find agreement between the physics of today and the postulations of the ancient scriptures.

Just as surely as an acorn planted in the soil is on its way to becoming a mighty oak, the reunion of each of us with our God Self is pre-ordained. It is not a question of "if" that reunion will take place, but "when."

I sometimes think of each human being as the heir to a royal throne who, at birth, developed amnesia and wandered off into a foreign land (populated with other amnesiacs). Not remembering who we truly are, we accept the beliefs of those around us, who are as deluded as we are. We have accepted the illusion that we are limited, powerless, alone, separate and unworthy. And then we spend our time and our energy attempting to overcome all those miserable limitations, struggling whole lifetimes to change the illusion.

Are You Ready to Wake Up?

The reality is that we don't need to change anything. All we need to do is wake up — wake up and realize that we have been suffering from a loss of memory. We have been asleep. We don't need to learn anything; we just need to remember what we have always known, and discover that we have nothing to attain, that we are already perfect.

The whole process, then, is a matter of becoming consciously aware of who you are . . . of realizing the true identity of your Self. Scientific Meditation is the simplest, fastest way to begin the journey back home to your Self.

8

Affirmation

"Man becomes what he believes himself to be.
If I keep on saying to myself that I can do a
certain thing, I shall surely acquire the capacity
to do it, even if I may not have it at the beginning."
Mahatma Gandhi

An affirmation is a powerful, positive statement. Always in the present tense, it means "to make firm or confirm." The use of affirmations is a vital element in the process of creatively changing your life, greatly reinforcing your efforts. Conscious affirmations, repeated with great mental attention and emotional conviction, cause a response in your body and mind via the medium of your subconscious mind. An even greater conscious focus in the repetition of affirmations reaches even beyond the subconscious to the super-conscious mind, which is a veritable storehouse of miraculous powers. When the affirmation reaches your superconscious mind, it releases a current of energy, which literally brings about a change in the psychophysiological habit pattern in your brain.

Importance of Self Talk

The very quality of your life is created to a great extent by the quality of your communication — with other people, yes, but more especially with yourself. How you talk to yourself about the events of your life determines your point of view and, thus, your experience. For example, a relocation to another city can be experienced in two vastly different ways. One person might lament, "This move is robbing me of all my close friends," while another might say, "How exciting! I will have the opportunity to meet many new people and some of them may turn out to be as close as my old friends!" Imagine how rich the quality of the latter attitude! Meeting that person certainly would be a different experience than meeting the first one, wouldn't it?

Affirmations are a potent, effective way of replacing old thoughts and beliefs that no longer serve you with positive ones of your choice. Once you pinpoint a negative thought, you can compose the affirmation which is the thought or belief you choose to have instead. Your focus, then, will be on the new thought you are programming, not on getting rid of the old one. It is counterproductive to resist an old thought. Instead, just turn your attention to the new one. Old thoughts and beliefs could be compared to a pitcher full of muddy water. Begin pouring in the clear, sparkling, fresh water of new thoughts and, eventually, there is no more muddy water left!

To work more effectively with affirmations, it is helpful to understand more about the way your mind functions. Computers are modeled after the human brain. If you have two computers that are built the same way, they will be able to perform the same way ,. provided they are programmed the same way. All human beings have the same neurology, the same nervous system and brain. It follows that what one person can do, any other person can do at least to some degree, *if the programming is the same!* Your thoughts and beliefs are simply the way you are programmed. If you had been born to parents of a different culture who spoke a different language with different belief systems, you would not have the thoughts and beliefs you have today. You would, instead, be a product of that other culture and language.

Thoughts and beliefs are a necessary part of life. They serve a good purpose, acting as a scaffolding during the construction period of your formative years, guiding you prior to the formation of a mature level of discrimination. But at a certain point, it is natural and useful to retire those thoughts and beliefs that no longer support the beautiful building of your life. Too often, however, the scaffolding becomes a prison, limiting your life experience. And, frequently, that prison is revered as sacred!

It is empowering to realize that thoughts and beliefs are entirely arbitrary; they are only the programming. And if one thought does not support what you want, you can plant a different thought, water it with your desire and harvest a correspondingly new experience.

A vital element in using affirmations successfully is repetitive practice which is long and deep enough to arouse strong belief. This taps the creativity of your life energy. (Observe that a doubt is a negative affirmation — it is a belief which is the opposite of faith!) Affirmations may be repeated silently, spoken out loud, written (including using a typewriter or word processor), sung alone or with other affirmations, or used as a chant. Chanting of affirmation is most effective when it begins at a normally audible volume and becomes more and more quiet until it becomes a silent chant deep within the mind.

Any positive statement can be an affirmation; you can easily compose your own. I have listed some here as examples.

1. The more I pay attention to what I want, the quicker it becomes a reality in my life.
2. My support is eternal and it comes from within.
3. Every day in every way I am getting better and better, happier and healthier!
4. I am a competent, reliable person and everyone knows it.
5. I do the work I love to do and and am rewarded lavishly for it!
6. Everything in my life always works out for the best, no matter what.
7. I am enjoying every moment of my life .
8. I easily express myself and when I speak, people hear me and understand my meaning.
9. I feel safe with other people and other people feel safe with me.
10. The longer I live, the happier and wiser I become.
11. The Light of God is creating miracles in my life.
12. I am a clear channel for the Heavenly Light.
13. I am an open channel for the riches of God.
14. The Light is flowing through me to create perfection in everything I do.
15. I open myself to the Light of the Universe.
16. The Light is pouring through me, healing my body, mind and emotions.
17. My connection to the Infinite Light provides me with everything I need or want in the moment I need or want it.
18. The Light is working through me silently to achieve its perfection.
19. I communicate clearly at all times.
20. The divine plan of my life is now revealed to me.

Using Affirmations

1. It is a good idea to work with at least one affirmation every day (since there is surely something you want to change!). And you can work with two or three affirmations if you wish. Remember, however, that it is better to truly focus on one and be effective and dynamic with that one — really create a change in your life — rather than attempt to do too much. If you feel you may dilute your attention, then stick to one at a time. You can use the affirmation many times during the day but be sure to use it during your visualization time and during the drowsy period when you are waking up and going to sleep.

2. Speak and write your affirmation in first person, then in second and third person. (Because you have been programmed from birth and even before birth, your unconscious mind may have accepted a thought or belief heard in second or third person. For example, "You're going to fall and hurt yourself" or "Susie gets sick so easily!")

First Person: " I, Jack, am prosperous and happy."
Second Person: "You, Jack, are prosperous and happy."
Third Person: "Jack is prosperous and happy."

3. *Written Affirmations with a Response Column*
On a piece of paper, draw a vertical line several inches from the right edge of the paper. You now have two columns on the paper — a wide one on the left and a narrow one on the right side. Write your affirmation in the left column. (Make sure you are breathing and allow yourself to experience the thoughts and feelings that are going on while you are writing.) Immediately write in the right column whatever thought you have. This will often be a negative thought or retort, which is

good because what you are doing is getting in touch with those negative thoughts and putting them on the paper. No matter how negative or disbelieving the response is initially, it will eventually become positive and accepting of the new thought or belief.

AFFIRMATION	RESPONSE
I have everything I need to do the things I want and everything I want to do the things I need.	Baloney!
I have everything I need to do the things I want and everything I want to do the things I need.	Who says?!
I have everything I need to do the things I want and everything I want to do the things I need.	Since When?
I have everything I need to do the things I want and everything I want to do the things I need.	Does this work?
I have everything I need to do the things I want and everything I want to do the things I need.	It would be great if this were true!
I have everything I need to do the things I want and everything I want to do the things I need.	I'm beginning to believe it!

4. Write your affirmation at least ten times a day for about 7 to 10 days. Then let it rest for a while and take effect. Do not judge whether or not it is working yet; just let it be and allow the changes. When you write a letter, you have to mail it or it will never reach its destination. In the same fashion, you must release the energy around your affirmation to reach its mark. In the meantime, it is okay to begin writing a different affirmation immediately while the first one is resting.

Written affirmations are effective because you are experiencing them both visually and kinesthetically (as you write or type on paper). To make them more memorable, you may wish to use different colored ink to write each one (red, green, blue, black). The right hemisphere of the brain recalls color and form so the additional element of color adds to the potency of the affirmation. You can create a poster using your favorite affirmation and give the letters unusual shapes and colors or decorate it vividly so your whole brain will "get it." (As an example, you can draw a big, red valentine heart around the word "love," a beautiful, yellow butterfly on the word "free" or a bold, green dollar sign next to the word "rich" in your affirmation.)

5. Speak your affirmation out loud while looking in the mirror. Repeat this several times and be sure to breathe during the process. Allow the new thought to sink into and permeate your consciousness. Smile and relax and begin feeling the feelings you will have when you have no trace of a doubt that the affirmation you have just spoken is entirely true. Become aware of your body posture. Stand the way you would stand if this affirmation were entirely true at this moment. Walk the way you would walk if you already had the thing you desire. Hold your head the way you would if you had already arrived at the place of realization of your affirmation. And keep breathing, connecting each inhale and exhale and allowing yourself to accept this new programming at every level: physical, emotional and mental.

Speak your affirmation aloud several times to a trusted friend, repeating it until the friend has the feeling that you really accept this new thought or belief. ("I am a confident, capable person.") Then ask your friend to speak your affirmation to you in the second person and again in third person, allowing yourself to really listen and absorb the sound and the message as you did when you were a child. ("Carol, you are a confident, capable person" and "Carol is a confident,

105

capable person"). Breathe deeply as you listen and take in the energy of this new thought.)

After a few repetitions, begin responding positively: ("Yes, you're right. I am a confident, capable person.") Keep breathing. Let the feeling sink in. Take all the time you need to truly absorb the new thoughts and feelings. Remember that you are reprogramming the film that is running through your projector; when the film is changed, the outpicturing on the screen of your life will change!

You are Telling The World What to Believe About You!

The world will believe about you whatever you truly believe about yourself. Every person and situation in your environment is really just holding up a big mirror to reflect back to you whatever you are sending out. What do you want the world to believe about you? Remember, your neurology is the same as that of everyone else; whatever anyone else can do, you can do, too. If you do not like your life, you can choose to change it!

9

Opening to Your Higher Self

"The highest revelation is that God is in every man."
Ralph Waldo Emerson

The experience of meeting your Higher Self is one of the most thrilling events of the inner journey. It is entirely natural and one often has a distinct feeling of having "come home" again. Many times when people experience this meeting for the first time, they think that they have met an angel or Christ or some other great master. The Higher Self is a presence of such radiance, purity and exaltation that a person often does not comprehend that it is a part of him or herself.

First contact with your Higher Self may include seeing a shaft of light, a Being of Light, or a diffused, radiant light. Some may feel or sense a loving, exalted presence without the visual experience. There may be dialogue with the Light or loving presence in the form of actual words or sentences and there is often a tremendously expanded experience of knowingness about many things - a sense of omniscience. Sometimes loved ones who have died will appear either alone or as part of a joyous, supportive group. You may experience scenes from or receive information about other lifetimes; usually, these past-life experiences will help you to clear or release some unconscious blockage which has limited you in some way.

Most people report that the fear of death disappears, replaced by the awareness that death is only a transition to another, usually freer, way of being. The sense of dissolving the narrow identity of self and melting into an expanded unity with all of life is experienced. There is a sense of being one with the essence of all other people and although this sense fades to some extent when the altered state closes up, the cellular and emotional memory of that experience creates a permanent change in one's neurology. There is often an awareness that we are only here to learn and that there is a specific purpose for this embodiment. After such an experience, people frequently devote themselves more selflessly to serving others. Money for money's sake or for the purpose of acquiring endless material possessions loses some of its attraction. A common element is the powerful conviction that love is all there is, that love is the essence of everything in the entire Universe, including human beings. One contact with your Higher Self will change your life forever.

"More than once when I sat all alone,
the mortal limit of the Self was loosed,
and passed into the nameless,
as a cloud melts into heaven."
    Alfred Lord Tennyson

After the first conscious contact with the Higher Self, a new way of living begins for the individual. Through meditation and communication with this higher level of being, the mind is fed with truth from within. This changes everything in the life of the person. Instead of the mind interacting with the external world almost exclusively, there now begins a vibrant infusion of life force from a higher plane and the person's focus shifts to include more of the higher vibration. The individual can then begin to put the goings-on of the lower, mundane world into proper perspective. He or she begins to move away from the old habits of the body and mind and to function from a place of alignment with the Soul. The individual begins to feel like a new person and operates less from compulsion and more and more out of conscious choice. A true spiritual empowerment of the person begins.

This part of yourself is the God part. It is your soul essence; it is what you truly are. We identify ourselves as the body, as the personality and as the conscious mind and we think we are separate from one another and separate from love. But we are essentially one and when we clear our consciousness of the blockages we carry (in the form of suppressed negative energy, false beliefs and judgments), we will discover that this blissful part has been inside all along.

Experiencing the Transition

The usual experience in the beginning is to open to the Higher Self only occasionally and sometimes to feel quite overwhelmed by the additional emotional and physical energy which accompanies this heightened state of awareness. It is an experience which is blissful beyond description, but because it is unfamiliar initially, some people attempt to hold it back because of this very newness, feeling some fear of the unknown.

This expansion will only occur when your ego structure is strong enough to survive the "breaking of the shell." You cannot surrender what you do not own; if the building of your ego is not yet sufficiently strong, you will not experience, through natural means, the dissolution of the boundaries we are discussing here.

Just a word here about drugs, especially hallucinogenics: Persons whose ego structures are relatively weak and still forming sometimes take drugs which prematurely force open the doors to expansion. Not only can this do physical and psychological damage, sometimes permanent, but it also may create a vulnerability to undesirable contacts with the astral world. Following natural methods, however, there is no danger. If a cocoon is opened artificially, even a day before its occupant is ready, death will occur. When the cocoon is naturally ready to open, the butterfly emerges delicate but strong. This contact with your Higher Self is an inevitable natural occurrence when you reach that point in your spiritual evolution.*

In your spiritual process of opening to your Higher Self, you may feel like you are "up" for a while, experiencing total connectedness and love for everyone and everything, and later feel as though you have been dropped back down to an old way of being, full of insecurity and feelings of separateness. It is not uncommon to feel somewhat confused by these shifts of consciousness. Let it be okay that you feel confused!

---

* A good analogy to spiritual evolution is to think of children in various grades in school. The essence and value of all children, from kindergarten to the higher grades, is the same: they all are human beings. But the ones in eighth grade function at a different level because they have experienced more learning and developed more complex abilities. It is, therefore, appropriate to have higher expectations of the eighth graders than of the younger children. So when we speak of a higher level of evolution, we are making distinctions about the development of the individual, not about their essence, which is divinity and is the same for all human beings. When a person experiences that "we are all one," it is this essential nature that he is experiencing.

In time, however, most people learn to open up to the energy of the Higher Self while continuing to function very capably in mundane matters and are increasingly able to move into contact with the Higher Self at will. At that point it often feels like having a dual awareness, one level being on a very exalted plane of consciousness and the other tending to business as usual.

In 1609, when Galileo observed that all the heavenly bodies he viewed through his telescope were round and, indeed, rotated around the Sun (just as Copernicus had postulated earlier), Galileo realized that Planet Earth is also round. Contrary to the popular belief of his day that the Earth was flat, this "truth" was not welcomed. In fact, he was regarded as a heretic! When accused by the powerful priests who wanted him tortured for heresy, he made a very practical appeal to them: "Don't take my word for it. Just look through the telescope and see for yourselves!" But the priests fearfully responded that to take even one look through Galileo's lens would indicate doubt in God and would, therefore, be a sin. (Besides, they already enjoyed immense power and exclusive status and saw no material advantage in allowing changes!) Thus reasoning, they refused to look through the telescope. They were accustomed to a "flat world" and resisted hearing about any further dimension, even if it might mean great enrichment in their lives.

This story about the closed minds of Galileo's day may seem ludicrous but it still applies to our world today. The content is different now, but the context is still pretty much the same. Today, we are accustomed to the world of three dimensions and often resist hearing about experiences beyond those three dimensions. But I want to encourage you to "look through the telescope." Stay open minded about the stories you are about to read; it can do no harm to at least reserve judgment until later, when you may have gained more personal experience.

The experience of the Higher Self takes place in the fourth dimension and beyond. As mentioned already, the energy of that Higher Self may take the form of images, sounds, words, telepathic communication, a sense of expanded knowingness, body feelings that communicate far more than one can comprehend and much more. The more openly accepting and child-like you can be in receiving these communications, the more easily they will flow into the channels of your awareness. In attempting to be "grown up," many people have lost contact with their inner child self. Much of my work with individuals and in workshops centers around the healing of the little inner child. Allowing this little child self its place of honor within is the direct route to accessing the Higher Self. This is what Jesus meant when He said, "Except you become as little children, you cannot enter the Kingdom of Heaven." (Matthew 18:3).

There is nothing new about the experiences described here. What is new is that greater numbers of people today are beginning to experience this natural expansion. This is the entire premise of Dr. Maurice Bucke's book, "Cosmic Consciousness," originally published in 1901, mentioned previously. And the scriptures of almost every religion include prophesies of a great outpouring of Spirit at some future time. The Old Testament prophet, Joel, functioning as a channel for the voice of the Divine, says, ". . .I will pour out My Spirit on all mankind; and your sons and daughters will prophesy; your old men will dream dreams; your young will see visions." (Joel 2:28)

Connection with the Higher Self in the form of a voice, a feeling, a visual image or any other form of awareness, has been experienced by countless people in history, from anonymous citizens to famous world leaders. Many of them have left written accounts describing these very personal experiences, including St. Paul, Francis Bacon, Walt Whitman, Edward Carpenter, Benedict Spinoza, Henry David Thoreau, Paramahansa Yogananda and St. Theresa of Avila. Dr. Carl Gustav Jung, whose work is such a priceless contribution to psychology today, said, "Often I had the feeling that I was no longer among men but was alone with God. I was outside time. I belonged to the centuries and He who gave answers was He who had always been."

George Washington's Vision

George Washington was encouraged by a powerful experience in expanded consciousness during the dark days of the American Revolution. On a sunny, cold day in the winter of 1777, he had remained alone at Valley Forge all afternoon.* When General Washington emerged from his quarters, looking pale and shaken, he seemed to feel a compulsion to share what was on his mind:

> "I do not know whether it is owing to the anxiety of my mind or what, but this afternoon as I was sitting at this table engaged in preparing a dispatch, something seemed to disturb me. Looking up, I beheld standing opposite me a singularly beautiful female. So astonished was I (for

---

* Anthony Sherman reported the story as it was originally told to him by General Washington. Many years later it was published by Wesley Bradshaw and has been reprinted from time to time since then. (Washington's Vision, National Tribune, Vol.4, No.12, December 1880.)

I had given strict orders not to be disturbed), that it was some moments before I found language to inquire the cause of her presence. A second, a third and even a fourth time did I repeat my question but received no answer from my mysterious visitor, except a slight raising of her eyes. By this time I felt strange sensations spreading through me. I would have risen but the riveted gaze of the being before me rendered volition impossible. I assayed once more to address her, but my tongue had become useless. Even thought, itself, had become paralyzed. A new influence, mysterious, potent, irresistible, took possession of me. All I could do was to gaze steadily, vacantly, at my unknown visitant. Gradually, the surrounding atmosphere seemed as though filled with sensations and grew luminous. Everything about me seemed to rarify, the mysterious visitor, herself, becoming more airy and yet more distinct to my sight than before, I now began to feel as one dying, or rather to experience the sensations which I have sometimes imagined accompany dissolution. I did not think, I did not reason, I did not move! All were, alike, impossible. I was only conscious of gazing fixedly, vacantly, at my companion.

"Presently I heard a voice saying, 'Son of the Republic, look and learn,' while at the same time my visitor extended her arm eastwardly. I now beheld a heavy white vapor rising at some distance, fold upon fold. This gradually dissipated and I looked upon a strange scene. Before me lay opened out in one vast plain all the countries of the world: Europe, Asia, Africa and America. I saw rolling and tossing between Europe and America the billows of the Atlantic and between Asia and America, lay the Pacific. 'Son of the Republic,' said the same mysterious voice as before, 'look and learn.'

"At that moment I beheld a dark, shadowy being like an angel, standing or rather floating in mid-air between Europe and America. Dipping water out of the ocean in the hollow of each hand, he sprinkled some upon America with his right hand, while with his left hand he cast some upon Europe. Immediately a cloud raised from these countries and joined in mid-ocean. For a while it remained stationery and then moved slowly until it enveloped America in its murky folds. Sharp flashes of lightning gleamed through it at intervals and I heard the groans and cries of the American people. A second time the angel dipped water from the ocean and sprinkled it out as before. The dark cloud was then drawn back to the ocean, in whose heaving billows it sank from view.

"A third time I heard the mysterious voice saying, 'Son of the Republic, look and learn.' I cast my eyes upon America and beheld villages and towns and cities springing up one after another until the whole land from the Atlantic to the Pacific was dotted with them. Again, I heard the mysterious voice say, 'Son of the Republic, the end of the century cometh! Look and learn.' At this, the dark shadowy angel turned his face southward and from Africa I saw an ill-omened specter approach our land. It flitted slowly over town and city. The inhabitants presently set themselves in battle array against one another. As I continued looking, I saw a bright angel on whose brow rested a crown of light on which was traced the word 'Union,' bearing the American flag, which he placed upon the divided nation and said, 'Remember we are all brothers.' Instantly, the inhabitants, casting from them their weapons, became friends once more and united around the national standard.

"And again I heard the mysterious voice saying, 'Son of the Republic, look and learn.' At this the dark shadowy angel placed a trumpet to his mouth and blew three distinct blasts and, taking water from the ocean, he sprinkled it upon Europe, Asia and Africa. Then my eyes beheld a fearful scene: From each of these countries arose thick black clouds which then joined into one and throughout this mass there gleamed a dark red light by which I saw hordes of armed men who, moving with the cloud, marched by land and sailed by sea to America, which country was enveloped in the volume of cloud. And I dimly saw these vast armies devastate the whole country and burn the villages, towns and cities that I beheld spring up. As my ears listened to the thundering of the cannon, the clashing of the swords and the shouts and cries of millions in mortal combat, I again heard the mysterious voice saying, 'Son of the Republic, look and learn.' When the voice had ceased, the dark shadowy being placed his trumpet once more to his mouth and blew a long and fearful blast.

"Instantly a light as of a thousand suns shone down from above me and pierced and broke into fragments the dark cloud which enveloped America. At the same moment, the angel upon whose head still shone the word, 'Union,' and who bore our national flag in one hand and a sword in the other, descended from heaven, attended by legions of white spirits. These immediately joined the inhabitants of America, who I perceived were well nigh overcome but who, immediately taking courage again, closed up their broken ranks and renewed their battle. Again amid the fearful noise of the conflict, I heard the mysterious voice saying, 'Son of the Republic, look and learn.'

"As the voice ceased, the shadowy angel for the last time dipped water from the ocean and sprinkled it upon America. Instantly the dark cloud rolled back, together with the armies it had brought, leaving the inhabitants of the land victorious. Then once more I beheld the villages, towns and cities springing up where I had seen them before, while the bright angel, planting the azure standard he had brought in the midst of them, cried with a loud voice, 'While the stars remain and the heavens send down dew upon the Earth, so long shall the Union last.' And taking from his brow the crown upon which blazoned the word, 'Union,' he placed it upon the standard while the people, kneeling down, said, 'Amen.'

"The scene instantly began to fade and dissolve and I at last saw nothing but the rising, curling vapor I had first beheld. This also disappearing, I found myself once more gaping upon the mysterious visitor who, in the same voice I had heard before, said, 'Son of the Republic, what you have seen is thus interpreted: Three great perils will come upon the Republic. The most fearful is the third, passing which, the whole world united shall not prevail against her. Let every child of the Republic learn to live for his God, his land and Union.' With these words the vision vanished and I started from my seat and felt that I had seen a vision wherein had been shown me the birth, progress and destiny of the United States."

In response to hearing an experience like this, the first question most of us want to ask is, "What exactly happened here?" We want so much to understand with our minds. We could speculate that perhaps the Higher Mind stimulated General Washington's brain to experience this vision internally. Or it could be that, if another person had been present on this occasion, he, too, could have seen it. How it happened seems unimportant. What is important is that this vision succeeded in giving Washington a glimpse of what lay ahead for America and left him better equipped to lead the young country. There was a definite and practical purpose served by this numinous experience, as there often is. On reading this account, one has little doubt that Washington was very inspired and quite transformed by the knowledge and assurances about the times which lay ahead. Trying to define in third-dimensional terms how this experience occurred, however, is attempting to understand the Infinite with the finite instrument of the little conscious mind. One would have as much success trying to measure the ocean using a teacup.

Like the vision of George Washington and the "voice" heard by Dr. Jung, the experiences described in the following chapter, both mine and those of others, do not fall within the framework of the third dimension and so I ask you to allow yourself to listen with the expanded awareness of your inner child self.

10

Experiences in
Expanded Consciousness

*"Such things have been revealed to me
that now all I have written appears in my
eyes as of no greater value than straw."*
St. Thomas Aquinas

At the end of the 19th Century, Dr. Bucke in <u>Cosmic
Consciousness</u> envisioned that increasing numbers of
men and women would experience the natural expansion in consciousness which he called "Cosmic Consciousness," presenting the personal case histories of
men and women who have experienced this phenomenon to a greater or lesser degree. Along with those
included therein, many more could now be listed.
Paramahansa Yogananda details many of his own
experiences in <u>Autobiography of a Yogi</u> and Sri Tara
Mata of Self-Realization Fellowship, in her booklet, "A
Forerunner of a New Race" presents the fascinating
story of her own experience of illumination. Dr. Bucke's
thesis that as mankind evolves, more and more people
are spontaneously experiencing this illumination, is
being borne out. As I travel around working with
various people, I see increasing evidence of it and I hear
questions and sometimes a degree of confusion about
what this means in the life of an individual.

Personally, I count as my greatest blessing the years
of firm foundation I gained through practice of Kriya
Yoga and adherence to the single-minded path of Self-
Realization. My spiritual identity was very strong and

deeply rooted before I began to experience the expansion written about below. Because of this, I have felt safe enough to feel the fear that is always present on moving into new and unknown territory and thus to allow the expansion and the new way of being it facilitates. I experience that I must continually locate and stay attuned to my "center," to keep my inner eye affixed to my guiding polestar, while I discover for myself just what the changes may mean. It could be compared to being continually refurbished from the inside out, an ongoing process of letting old, outworn thoughts and habits go, making room for the new. I know that I feel like an entirely different person than I felt just a few years ago. I observe that I now function comfortably in ways that are way beyond what I could have managed even a short time ago.

Dr. Bucke observed that one must not suppose that because a man or woman has the illumining experience of expanded consciousness, that that person is, therefore, omniscient or infallible. He pointed out that these people are in a sense (though on a higher plane of being) like children who have just become self conscious — a period of time is required for the child to adjust and adapt himself before he can become masterful at the new, higher level.

I observe that my experiences and those of many others are natural occurrences, a result of having reached a sufficiently high level of development in the cerebro-spinal centers to facilitate this higher experience. The challenge for each of us is to find out what it means and specifically how to work in alignment with it for the highest good of all. Indeed, it is consistent that when one experiences this awakening, that he or she begins to feel an inner soul yearning that cries out to be utilized by the Divine. "Thy Will Be Done" becomes the intense, energized, passionate motto of these newly awakened ones, a result of that individual's inner experience alone, quite apart from any religious context. I see these experiences, then, not as religious experiences, but as human experiences. The natural outcome of an evolving human being is finally Cosmic Consciousness!

My Own Experiences

I was participating in an intense workshop when my breathing changed, becoming deeper and fuller. I ceased being aware of my external surroundings because suddenly there was so much going on in my internal awareness — it was as if suddenly there was a movie inside but at the same time it was live and I was part of it. And these inner occurrences were so full of energy that I was caught up completely in them. Because of this intense energy, they seemed much more real than what was occurring in my outer experience in the room.

I suddenly became aware that in my inner experience, I was in a different place, a tunnel in which I had been trapped in a horrible, recurring nightmare which I began experiencing in very early childhood and which had recurred frequently all my life.*

Here is my dream: "I am very small and inside a tunnel of some kind. I want to get out the end of the tunnel. My mother and father are outside and I want to get out to them and safety, but there is something in front of me which is keeping me from getting out.

---

* (I have been reluctant to write about this dream because of its bizarre and frightening nature, but I keep waking up at 4:00 in the morning with a strong urge to set it into writing. Finally I realize that it is appropriate for me to tell this story and I am now willing to stop resisting it. Perhaps it will serve someone in ways I do not know.)

Whatever this 'something' is, it seems as big as I am and I have to push it out before I can get out. I push and push and it does seem to move a little bit, but I get nowhere.

"I am desperate to get out because 'the devil is in there' with me. He is behind me somewhere and I am utterly, literally horrified; I feel sheer terror go up my spine. The fear is so great that I do not believe any words could describe it. I must get away; I must get out of there and away from him!"

And the nightmare would always end right there. Often I would awake suddenly, terrified, and feel the shock of adrenalin that accompanies extreme, sudden fear. When I finally told someone about this nightmare (for the very first time in my life!) I was in my twenties. After that, I never had the nightmare again.

Ten years later, I was participating in an intensive workshop, which combined the elements of Gestalt, primal scream and connected breathing. I was already well acquainted with connected breathing (rebirthing), having begun to experience its powerful healing, clearing effects a year before. During more than ten years of meditation and that year of rebirthing, I had experienced altered states many times and was not afraid of the increased physical, emotional and psychic energy which accompanies such states. The participants in this workshop (those who were courageous enough) were each working on their own very basic issues, which almost always involve terror. That primal fear functions like vicious wolves guarding those core issues, holding at bay anyone who would attempt to approach. This effectively keeps us away from dealing with those issues and preserves the cell of fear, keeping it intact and very powerful. It is all the more powerful because it is unconscious — for the most part, a person does not consciously realize it is there! But the time comes when, under the guidance and protection of the Higher Self, one becomes brave enough to face the primal terror and proceed toward it, willing at last to confront all the demons lurking in the inner darkness, preferring to die to the physical, if that occurs, rather than be ruled any longer by fears that imprison the spirit!

Suddenly my breathing stopped, which was a very expanded feeling, and in my inward experience I felt: "I am back in the terrifying nightmare!" After a short time, my breathing resumed but I was still in the tunnel. As soon as possible, I asked for help. A skilled facilitator was able to assist, asking,

"WHERE ARE YOU?"

"In the womb." (As I heard myself say this, it was the very first time I ever realized that the tunnel was either the womb or the birth canal.

"WHAT ARE YOU FEELING?"

"I'm terrified!"

"OF WHAT?"

"The Devil is in here with me."

"WHERE IS HE?"

"Behind me."

"TURN AROUND AND LOOK. . ."
(I did) . . ."WHAT DO YOU SEE?"

"Nothing!"

"THEN WHAT IS IT?"

"It's a thought . . .it's a belief!"

"YEAH ...WHOSE THOUGHT IS IT?"

"It's their belief, my parents, my father."

"OKAY ... AND WHO ELSE"

"Me! It's my belief! I took on his belief!"

"THAT'S RIGHT. IT'S YOUR BELIEF NOW.
YOU HAVE BEEN CARRYING THIS THOUGHT
AROUND SINCE BEFORE YOU WERE BORN.
THAT'S WHY YOU'VE ALWAYS BEEN SO CARE-
FUL TO BE SUCH A GOOD GIRL -- YOU WERE
AFRAID OF THIS THOUGHT."

   "So now what can I do?"
"YOU MUST OWN THAT THIS IS IN THERE - YOU
MUST OWN THAT THIS IS YOUR THOUGHT, YOUR
FEAR NOW."

I began moaning and screaming with the pain and anguish I felt. Every exhalation became a scream. As I continued to scream, the thought form began leaving. I could feel a dark blue energy — each time I screamed, it felt like a little more of it left me. It was like a dark mist and each scream vented more of it as it left me bit by bit. After screaming for a few minutes, I felt emptied, drained, exhausted, limp. Everyone in the workshop (they were supporting my process) probably felt rather drained at that point. The Facilitator completed this part of the process by asking several other participants to take care of me and announced a 3-hour break. My friends took me to the Ocean and led me into the water so I could walk around and "ground myself" for a while. I felt very childlike, and they took care of me like a child. I felt my consciousness tremendously expanded. I could see auras around people and trees and over the water. I felt total, unconditional love for everyone and everything I glanced at or thought about!

   When the workshop resumed later that evening, a lady with whom I felt great rapport and compassion was the first to sit in the "hot seat," our name for the chair in which one sat to deal with fear, etc. She was working on trauma that had occurred when she was a tiny child, which was very frightening and painful for her. Feeling love for her and a desire for her to experience healing, I was sitting on the floor, intensely focused on her process, and still in that state of great expansion which had begun hours before.* Suddenly, without warning, my conscious awareness shifted to another place, like a channel was suddenly changed on an inward TV screen. (I was later told that my body slumped over to the floor and that I was carried to another part of the room, laid on the carpeting and covered with a blanket.)

Though I was lying down physically, in my inner experience I was standing up. Standing immediately in front of me, just inches away with its back to me, was an enormous creature — a black angel! It had wings and feathers which were so black they glistened purple in the sunlight. It was huge, about 7 feet tall. Its shoulders, above and immediately in front of my line of vision, towered above me, over the top of my head. This black, winged creature was standing so close that when I breathed out, the air from my exhalation rustled the edges of the feathers! I felt practically paralyzed with fear! It is an understatement to say that I wanted it to leave me! Oh! How I wanted to push it away from me! But I also knew, somehow, that physical strength would have no effect on this creature, this black angel Devil. I knew intuitively that I must use my will to force it away from me. (It was not a physical creature and could not be vanquished with physical energy!)

*The absence of self-consciousness, as when one is entirely attentive to someone else, seems to allow the dissolution of the ego boundaries as related here. It is as though my consciousness expanded out beyond the identification with the little self to identify with the greater whole which includes other people. Only in this state of expansion can humans truly experience unconditional love. It is, then, a loving of one's greater Self.

I began to use my will to send energy out from the Christ Center (the mid-spot between the eyebrows) to push this creature away from me. At first there was no movement. I felt panic. Not knowing what else to do, I kept using my will and gradually it began to move forward away from me very slowly. I was very encouraged by even the small amount of movement and began to use my will even more strongly. The movement of the creature away from me gained momentum.

As the distance increased, the speed also increased. Finally, when it had moved about 300 yards from me, I was able to push it over a cliff, using only the force of my will. For a second, I stood motionless, afraid it was too good to be true that this "thing" was really gone! Then I ran to the edge of that cliff and looked down. There, spread-eagled on the beach below, lay the horrible black angel. It was totally still. Was it dead? Some part of me feared that this "thing," not being human in the first place, could not be killed! I was afraid it would get up. I was afraid it would regain some of its power. I tried to imagine somehow that it was gone, but it would still be lying there when I looked again. So I kept a watch on it from the cliff high above to make sure it did not move.

I felt empty, emptied out inside. I had never felt like that before in my life. Suddenly in my inner experience, the channel shifted again and I was lying on something like a hospital gurney in a corridor. There was a beautiful shaft of light above me about four feet wide. It was the most radiant, most alive substance I have ever seen, yet it wasn't at all blinding. I knew that I wanted to fill myself with light from the shaft of light which was hovering above me. I called Paramahansa Yogananda to "come to me and fill me with the light," a silent, telepathic call. Yoganandaji* appeared and stood at my left side. Taking a few steps, he drew up very close to me, almost touching my left arm. He stood there at my side for a few moments, then stepped back and stood a few feet away, patiently watching me. But he did not fill me with the light! His presence was supportive but a little detached; I was receiving his love although he did not verbally express it. I did not understand this and felt a little confused. As he continued to stand on my left, silently supportive, I called for Christ to "come and fill me with the light."

Christ appeared and approached on my right side, took a few steps toward me, coming up very close for a few moments, then moved back a few feet and stood on my right side, silently loving and supporting me but, like Yogananda, Christ did not fill me with the light either! Lying there, empty and waiting, feeling a child-like trust, I looked at both Yogananda and Christ, standing on my left and right, respectively, and wondered what was going to happen.

Then Yoganandaji spoke, "You can go direct now." As I heard these words, I understood that I was to be responsible for filling myself with the light. But how, I wondered? In this state of consciousness, asking a question mentally seems to be sufficient and an immediate answer came to me. I knew instantly that I was to use my will to fill myself with the Light, drawing it in through the Christ Center. Immediately I began to draw in the light. It seemed to take a long time although I don't know how long it actually was in clock time. I felt that every cell had to be full of the White Light and I didn't want to stop until I felt completely satisfied that this was done. Finally I felt luminous and radiant and full of White Light.

*"ji" is a Sanskrit suffix indicating reverence and respect.

Then the most remarkable thing happened: the Shaft of Light began to talk to me! It said, "I'm going to do everything from now on!" Such a simple sentence but the meaning expanded out in waves in my consciousness like water expanding in circles around the entry point of a rock. I instantly realized that this Light had always done everything, only I had not known it! I wondered if it could really be this simple, if I could actually surrender the "doing" to the Higher Presence, and asked, "What do I have to do?" I think I was expecting a list but the answer was simply, "Just stay in your integrity, every moment, to the best of your ability." Another smooth pebble tossed into the lake of my expanding awareness!

Again, in waves, I instantly understood paragraphs - maybe even volumes - of what was meant by "integrity," far more than any dictionary definition. It was just as clear that the guidance given was for me, and might or might not apply to any other person. A significant conviction was that one meaning of integrity means following the perfect inward guidance Spirit communicates to each person. The problem is that until a person has become sufficiently clear and receptive, the inner voice of guidance goes unheard. Like tuning into a single, clear voice in a shouting mob, the Higher Self or Holy Spirit, though always present and available, cannot be heard until the noisy crowd of negative beliefs, especially fear, guilt, judgment and self-righteousness, is cleared out!

With one fell swoop this awareness obviated to me the inevitability of going beyond religion. Religion is a standardizing of one person's experience and applying it to many others, with subsequent value judgments of right and wrong and a disregard for the direct connection each person can achieve. When human beings are functioning fully, there is no need to universalize any individual message for "we each become our own messenger." The original form of guidance, built into our circuitry, is the inner guidance which is always perfect for each of us and may or may not apply to any other person, including even our own children. Religion can serve, just as scaffolding can serve to build a building. But, having served its purpose, it is appropriate to remove it and set it aside or at least to recognize that it is the building, itself, which has value, and not the scaffolding! The scaffolding isn't wrong; it is just that having served its purpose well, it isn't needed anymore! It is lovely to enjoy church ritual but is misleading to confuse the ritual or the form, with the essence!

Another strong conviction of yet another meaning of integrity was to tell the truth about everything all the time, including especially to tell myself the truth about what I am really feeling in each moment. To gloss over a feeling in order to "be nice," is out of integrity. (Not that I have to tell anyone else - maybe so or maybe not depending on the circumstances - but it was made clear to me that I must do my best to tell myself the truth.) Hiding from what I really feel would be to allow static to muffle the beautiful, clear voice of the Light.

This dialogue with the Light continued for a time; I was given personal assurances and more information including a fail-safe way (a physical "anchor") to reconnect quickly to this state of awareness at any time no matter what the circumstances. Finally, the experience feeling complete, I heard a strong, telepathic communication, "You have a new covenant now!" A new covenant; a new way of being. Clearly, the old way of functioning would work no longer. I now had new promises, newly-found support and certainly I had new responsibilities.

I know the above process may seem bizarre, but stay with me. In the days which followed this experience, I was given much intuitive understanding regarding this, including the following:

1. The Bible Belt culture and the Pentecostal Church, which had a great influence on my family, contains a lot of judgment and fear regarding sexuality. (They have no corner on that market, of course; witness the widespread attitude that a "dirty" joke is a sexual one.) At the moment of orgasm, sensually pleasurable though it is, there is also a simultaneous sense of guilt, because of this unconscious judgment. The most vital substances in human male and female are sperm and ovum, veritably packed with sufficient life force energy to form a new human being and sustain the life force in that person for a whole incarnation - in other words, sperm and ovum are extremely alive! An infant's womb life begins through this act which so many people have (at least unconsciously) judged as "sinful." The vital soul coming into that fertilized cell is pure consciousness itself, and perceives at a deep, core level these thoughts, feelings and judgments. In my super-expanded awareness in the experience described above, I could feel the energy of those fears and judgments. This is another confirmation of how very conscious we are (even at conception!) and how clearly the forming child perceives the thoughts and feelings, especially of parents. How painful judgment is! No wonder Christ forbade it.

2. In the Pentecostal Church, there are frequent frightening references to the Devil, replete with vivid descriptions of the Devil being a "fallen angel," a "dark angel," etc. Children are usually present when these fearful sermons are threateningly delivered with great emotional fervor to believing audiences. Apparently ignorant of the harm it causes, parents reinforce these concepts and frightening images, giving implied approval by their silence. Such church attendance by little ones, then, instills not faith but fear (the opposite of love).

I listened to countless such descriptions, feeling afraid and unsafe, using my excellent child's imagination to create an exact thoughtform which, unknown to me until the experience described above, resided ominously in my unconscious mind. I believe that the "black angel devil" took the form I experienced because that is the exact picture I had imagined while listening to those vivid descriptions and then unwittingly accepted it into my consciousness as a young child. And, of course, it had to go into my unconsciousness; it was much too terrifying to hold in my conscious awareness!

I wish to add here that regardless of what one believes the theological facts to be, it does only harm to present such fearful subject matter to children, perhaps even more harm than allowing children to watch frightening, evil images on television. I would appeal to all parents and other adults to take it upon themselves to deal in a loving, healthy and responsible way with children, seeking always to empower young ones to reach for their highest potential expression. Children are so trusting and impressionable and they usually accept as true whatever respected elders present to them. To handicap a child with fearful imaginings contributes not to autonomy and sound mental health but to psychological and emotional imbalance.

3. Since the above experience, I have felt such clarity that self-condemnation is a direct violation of the Holy Spirit within each of us. One has no right to condemn himself. Only the frightened, separate ego mind would have the audacity to judge and always it is the Holy Spirit within which is judged. Human beings have been so programmed to condemn themselves and feel guilty that in many cases, a person is unaware he is doing so. It is urgently important to begin to become conscious about this subject and begin the process of forgiving self and releasing the old, painful habits of guilty self-condemnation. Guilt does not prevent further error; on the contrary, it attracts further error! The appropriate and powerful way to deal with any error is to learn your lesson as quickly as possible, then to forgive and love yourself and go

on. This way, the Holy Spirit can resume and continue its unimpeded and glorious expression through you.

This experience was a feeling of being one with Love and Light. I experienced that I Am the Light, that I am Love and that Love and Light, Liquid Light, are all the same thing. And I know these words don't make any sense in a three-dimensional, mental way. This kind of experience occurs in the fourth-dimension or beyond and third-dimensional mentality is not capable of understanding or experiencing anything beyond itself. Just as you cannot be in Canada and the USA at the same moment, you cannot be in the third dimension and the fourth simultaneously. The best you can do is bring back to the third dimension a vivid memory of the higher experience.

But once you visit that higher dimension, you will always be able to go back there again. It could be compared to riding a bike: once you succeed in balancing and riding for even a short distance, you can always do it again! Perhaps a new neuron pathway is opened up and programmed with the new experience, a new corridor for reaching the vast banquet hall of Spirit. One experience in this dimension is life changing. It is a reconnection to the Higher Self, to the Intuition, which will begin to guide your life.

This experience embodies a special thrill of ecstasy for me, although every such experience is indelibly imprinted in my consciousness. Your own experience of Light or Spirit awaits you; it is natural, it is that arrival at a certain point of evolution you will reach when you are ready. This is the experience of reunion with Spirit. Without this experience, you cannot help but feel separate — the third dimension is capable of nothing more than separate feeling. However, with even the first excursion into the heaven of the fourth dimension, some part of you will always know that you are essentially not separate but that we are all one!

In the days which followed the experience described above, along with the joy and love which I felt, I continued to keep my inward vigil from the top of the cliff. The black angel still lay perfectly still below. One morning I awoke in the wee hours, feeling renewed terror that this creature was not dead but would arise to haunt me again. I felt like a tiny baby (indeed I perceive that when we are truly frightened, we usually do regress to a very infantile state of consciousness, where rational thinking has no power). I realized that I must have help and called my rebirther, Dr. Sonia Powers, who had supported me so lovingly in the intensive workshop experience. Someone drove me to her home (I felt too perturbated to drive) and she spent the day with me, loving me unconditionally, rebirthing me, assuring me and helping me to heal. I felt fortunate and blessed to have a knowledgeable, loving person to help me through this very critical time. It was this single day, more than any other experience, which allowed me to see the great value of a loving, skilled rebirther. At one point, we went down to the beach where the creature lay motionless and used a laser gun to vaporize it. It disappeared completely (and permanently!) except for the tiniest dot left in the sand. It bothered me that even that dot remained; Sonia assured me that the dot would always serve me as a reminder of the whole victorious experience. By the end of the day I felt very free, happy and "grown up again!"

This experience took place, from start to finish, over a period of about a week and seemed to signal the beginning of a phase of greatly accelerated psychological and spiritual growth in my life. I sometimes think I could write a whole volume just recounting the inner experiences of that spring and summer. But that is not the purpose of this present book so I will limit my personal stories to just a few. One of the most remark-able after that involved my name. (Christina is the name given me by my Higher Self.) The experiences surrounding this name were so unusual and uplifting to me that I want to share them with you here.

A New Name

As mentioned before, I have experienced the inner presence throughout my life; I cannot recall any signifi-cant span of time when it was absent. Frequently this presence makes itself known as a voice. Most of the time, it comes in the form of sudden ideas and flashes of knowingness. (I usually become aware, later, that some inspiration has come through but at the time of occurrence, I am not objectively aware that I am channelling.) One of its distinct characteristics is a marked absence of self-consciousness and there is always a sense of total inner absorption. These experi-ences are remarkable enough, yet sometimes the inner voice becomes even more distinct, communicating in a powerful, audible way, as though someone else is speaking in fully-formed sentences. It is always clear to me that this is not an external voice that someone else nearby could hear, yet it is audible to me just the same.

On these occasions it seems as if the voice is coming from another presence, a loving higher presence, and I always feel "stopped in my tracks." This second kind of experience is marked by the same total absorption and lack of self-consciousness and, additionally, by a greatly increased amount of physical and emotional energy in my body and awareness. It feels ecstatic and nearly overwhelming at times. It is this second type of experience that I want to share with you here regarding my name.

At birth I was given a first name which was never used; instead, I was called by my middle name, which is Joan. Years later after I was well along on my spiritual path, (several months after the black angel experience), the inner voice began stating, "Your name is Christina". And again the next day, "Your name is Christina." This experience continued for a period of some weeks; I kept silent, mentioning it to no one.

Finally, one day when my daughter and I were driving along the highway, I asked, casually, "Do you like the name 'Christina?'" She was only 9 years old then and ordinarily wanted no changes in her mother, so I was surprised when she gushed: "Oh, Mom, I love that name! Are you going to change your name to Christina? Oh, Mom, please do! I think it is beautiful and it fits you!" I was genuinely surprised by her enthusiasm! I hadn't said a word about changing my name! But I have experienced many times that children speak for Spirit and felt this might be a confirmation of the inner message I was receiving.

I recalled reading that some people undergo a name change when they advance sufficiently along a spiritual path, as a way of acknowledging the new person inside. I knew that a number of Biblical characters received new names, among them Abraham, Sarah, Peter and Paul. And monastics usually receive a spiritual name on initiation. Maybe I had outgrown my present name. A week later the powerful inner voice spoke again: "Begin using your new name today!" The direction was so strong and I felt such congruence in my body that I had no doubt at all and immediately obeyed.

A few weeks later, I went to the California Department of Motor Vehicles to change my name on my driver's license. I completed the form, changing "Joan" to "Christina" and got into the line to await my turn. Suddenly I felt an enormous sadness welling up from within. I began breathing and allowing the feeling to permeate my body, recognizing that something suppressed was coming up into my conscious awareness. Within seconds, the message was unmistakable: The little inner child, Joan, was feeling unloved, discarded and unappreciated. It felt like she was crying out, "I have done the best I could — I got us *this* far!" A veritable storm of emotion was now seething inside me and I put on sunglasses to hide eyes too full of tears for a public place! Receiving that communication, I knew what I had to do: I quickly changed the printed form to read "Christina Joan." Christina would replace my old, unused first name and Joan would remain my middle name!

Now it was my turn at the window. The necessary paperwork completed, I turned and literally ran to my car, feeling waves of emotion washing over me like the surf. Safely seated in the privacy of my car, great heaving sobs overtook me and I continued to breathe as best I could and to stay attuned to the overwhelming feelings. Suddenly, in inward vision, I saw an image of a little wooden boat, like a rowboat, being placed onto the deck of a large, white ship. The moment the little boat was in place, the ship launched out into the waters with a swoosh! I felt my whole being carried along with the movement of that ship. And I knew that the little boat was "Joan" and the white ship was "Christina."

Midst the emotional tumult inside, the inner voice spoke again, explaining, reassuring, like a protective parent, "The little boat couldn't handle the waters we are moving into now!" I felt total, unconditional love. The boundaries of my little separate self completely dissolved in a torrent of ecstatic gratitude and a feeling of safety, protection and connectedness as I realized that the little boat, the personal self, was being protected and carried along safely inside the great, white ship, a more transpersonal self.

I breathed and continued to allow the extra life force into and through my body and awareness. As joyful as it was, it was yet all I could do to "hang on." Only by totally surrendering to the energy with no idea where it was taking me could I flow along with the process. Actually, it felt much more like riding the rapids than flowing along! Nothing less than total trust in the intelligence and love of the Universe was necessary for me to stay with this process. And I reflected to myself that anyone who thinks that the spiritual life is boring hasn't come anywhere close to experiencing this!

A little later the beloved voice spoke again, triumphantly, "See, I can use almost anything to teach you!" More tears. An entire transformation had occurred; a new paradigm was now in place. Something was occurring that was bigger than I could consciously grasp, carrying me victoriously with it, and I did not even have to understand it! Good thing! It was crystal clear I had no model for understanding this! Maybe understanding has really been greatly overrated anyway!

As soon as I recovered enough to drive, I went home and got into the hot tub. For the next two hours, I breathed and went back to my conception and assured the tiny embryonic baby, Joan, that she would always be safe and loved and appreciated. I then moved forward to my birth, and repeated the assurance process with the newborn child. Then to my first birthday and second birthday and so on until I had reached my current age. Stopping at each birthday, I acknowledged the little inner child for doing her best, for her integrity, for her willingness to be open and to learn, even when it felt unsafe at times to do so. I expressed my appreciation to her over and over and thanked her "for having gotten us this far." Finally, my body and psyche felt completely peaceful and joyful in every way.

Having experienced all of this regarding my name, I have felt totally congruent with the change. Never for one moment have I felt uncertain about it in any way. Several years later, I went to court to have "Christina" become my legal first name and felt, again, the joyful celebration that has surrounded this experience from the beginning. My feeling, now, is that the first name given me at birth served just to "hold the space" for my true name, which I had to grow into. When I reached a certain point in my spiritual evolution, it was timely and appropriate to take my new name. And at that time, my Higher Self communicated to me very clearly what that name was and when to begin using it. I have experienced a number of times since that "Christina" can function in ways that "Joan" alone would be unable to do, and the image of the little wooden boat and the white ship returns to my inner vision.

On occasion, the expansion in consciousness occurs in dramatic ways, as related above; at other times, it is momentous because of its very simplicity. Early on a recent, cold November morning, I went out into my neighborhood for a brisk, two-mile walk. After I had walked about half a block, I suddenly realized that there was light everywhere! Light, a glowing, luminescent, light was emanating from each bare branch and bush. It was not at all just a visual experience; this radiant light, shimmering everywhere as though in a vibrational dance of atoms, was so alive that it felt like love everywhere! I felt my emotional and egoistic boundaries give way as they have many times on such blessed occasions. Tears streaked down my face throughout the whole walk that singular morning. Rather than walking, I felt like liquid moving through liquid, like love moving through love, for indeed it felt like melting and becoming one with all surroundings. As early morning drivers hurried by, ignoring me (for which I was very grateful), I felt a space of divine love with the being behind each wheel, without any need to know anything more about them!

Another time I experienced the spontaneous expansion in consciousness at a wedding reception. Sitting at a table with my daughter and a friend, I looked up at the bride and groom as they were chatting with wedding guests. Suddenly it was as though it was not I who was seeing them but Divine Mother (God in the aspect of Mother). For what was probably about a minute or two, I sat transfixed in this gaze of utter, unconditional love which focused first on the wedding couple, then expanded to include everyone present in the reception hall. Then the only way I can describe what happened next is that it felt like "Divine Mother let me see, too!" At that moment, I, Christina, became aware of this vast, sweet, all-encompassing total love. I thought to myself, "Oh! I knew Divine Mother loves us, but I never imagined it was this intense!" (The inner awareness I received was that in the first minute or two, none of my self-consciousness was present and the experience was purely that of "Divine Mother seeing." Then some small portion of my self-consciousness returned — enough for my separate ego-mind to become aware in an objective way that this was happening through me and it felt like "Divine Mother let me see, too!")

One remarkable element of the experiences in expanded consciousness is that no matter how many times I have experienced such states, each one is vibrantly alive, powerful and transformative. The expanded state is familiar now but it never becomes even the slightest bit ordinary. The experience of total love lingers more and more, transforming everyday consciousness, but at every moment seems to me "priceless beyond all imagination." Yoganandaji often referred to God as "ever-new joy," a fitting description. Unlike the treasures of the world, there is no tendency to look beyond for something better. This union in expanded consciousness, then, is the ultimate prize.

I hope that sharing these experiences will encourage you to follow your inner guidance, even if it seems a little outrageous at times, thus allowing your inner teacher to lead you more easily on the grand adventure of your life. We all have a higher calling and must be able and willing to have the little self surrender to the expansion and alignment with the Higher Self in order to fully answer that call.

I have included here some actual stories of other people who have experienced an expansion within themselves. Except in obvious cases, the names have been changed. These accounts are reprinted here in the words of those individuals.

Sharon D. Gary, M.S.

"I am a Psychological Examiner in private practice for a number of years. Because of my professional training, I have long had more than my share of intellectual knowledge and understanding of the effects on a child of early family dynamics, including especially my own traumatic experiences in a dysfunctional family. Insight alone, however, did not correct the underlying emotional attitudes I had formed about myself and my life. I had become increasingly aware that I had unfinished emotional business left over from my childhood. With growing frequency I would go home after a day of psychotherapy with clients to look at myself in the mirror and feel like a fraud because I felt so empty myself. How could I help others heal if I could not heal myself? I didn't know where to turn. Because I was already experiencing that an abundance of intellectual insight did not bring healing, I was reluctant to acquire still more insight by re-entering a psychotherapeutic process. What I wanted and needed was not more insight but a sense of wholeness.

"In doubt how to proceed, I turned to God, asking to be made whole on all levels of my being; in return I would do whatever God required to accomplish this and I would give joyfully of my money and time. Shortly afterwards, in late 1986, I met Christina and began rebirthing sessions with her. I also participated in an intensive transformational workshop which Christina facilitated and during which I volunteered to undergo a period of isolation and subsequent presentation of an emotional autobiography.

"Those rebirthing sessions and the workshop experience were instrumental in my healing process. I re-experienced events from my birth and childhood which produced corrections in my emotional patterns. While I knew the details of my birth and childhood on a cognitive level, until Christina worked with me I had felt none of the feelings and, of course, this was the necessary ingredient in bringing about my healing. I could then clearly see my original faulty perceptions, judgments and, especially, guilt. This new knowingness allowed me to forgive myself and others. It allowed me to love myself more fully and, thereby, to accept love more fully from others, including God. This produced healing and a sense of wholeness.

"Let me describe the rebirthing sessions. The first time I, apparently, had some unconscious resistance for I managed to get lost on the way to our appointment, though I supposedly knew the way. I persevered and Christina graciously agreed to see me, though it was late. That resistance conquered for the moment, we settled down and Christina explained the connected breathing procedure. It sounded simple enough and I felt comfortable in the surroundings and with Christina.

"After just a few minutes, the breathing became more difficult for me but I persevered. Later (it seemed like a long time later) I felt that nothing was happening. I wondered what to do. I did not want to hurt Christina's feelings by telling her that this was not working and I didn't know enough about the process to fake it. What was I to do?

"As I pondered these thoughts with my conscious mind, I had kept up the breathing. Before I reached a decision about my dilemma, my body began to assume a fetal position. I was shocked to observe this but was unable to stop it. I hoped Christina wouldn't notice. She noticed. After that, I felt like I was on a slide, unable to stop or turn back as I re-experienced the events leading up to my birth and the first few days of infancy. I saw, heard, felt and knew what was happening at each point. Let me try to describe this for you.

"After my body assumed the fetal position, my toes became numb. The numbness slowly spread upward and, as it reached my waist, I became aware that I was going to die. This thought produced no panic or fear, just calm acceptance. Then, almost instantly, I felt cold and blinded by bright lights at the same time that I felt a heavy weight on my chest, keeping me from breathing for a long time. (This is truly remarkable for I have never, ever been able to hold my breath.) I then felt something warm over my body and then someone did something to my mouth which I did not like and I began to sob and cry.

"Blood was everywhere and my mother wasn't moving. I heard myself scream out, 'Oh God! I've killed my mother!' Then I was taken away from her by cold, disapproving people. (I was an illegitimate child and my birth was in a small-town hospital where even the medical staff knew of the circumstances and disapproved and judged the situation.) I knew they did not approve of me. They did not answer my cries and fears about my having killed my mother. They just put me in a small space and left me alone. I cried briefly then felt, 'It's okay; I'm okay; I can breathe.' Then I quietly waited.

"The nurses cared for me, but with distance and disapproval. Later some strangers came to take me. I wasn't ready to go yet because breathing was difficult outside my little space but I knew I had to go because these people were my punishment for killing my mother.

"This experience answered many questions surrounding my birth. Friends had noticed certain peculiarities such as my inability to hold my breath, my morbid fear of pregnancy and particularly of childbirth, my early uneasiness around babies, and my frequent complaints of feeling smothered in close emotional relationships. I realized why I had dreaded intimacy, for I feared that anyone who got too close to me would either leave me or be hurt by me. Others had commented that I seemed to have a high level of guilt, although I felt none consciously. The experience of realizing that as a newborn I thought I had killed my

143

mother explained this deep-seated and enormous guilt. Re-experiencing these events allowed me to release old faulty perceptions, judgments and self-condemnation and, therefore, to forgive myself.

"My second rebirthing session was less dramatic, but allowed me to experience my soul behind my heart and my connection with Christ and God and, indeed, with all living beings. I experienced such profound joy and love and peace that no words could describe it. I left the second session feeling like I had come home and was now whole. This wholeness has never left me and I have never felt alone or empty since then."

John Colton, Attorney

"I have been aware of an inner divine presence or Higher Self all my life. The levels of this awareness, however, have changed. As a child I carried on a dialogue with this inner presence until I was told this was 'crazy.' The church taught that God was 'out there.' Thereafter, I prayed to God in heaven and, although I was somewhat comfortable with this, I had grown uneasy about my relationship with a fearful God. In recent years, I have had experiences that have shown me I have a loving friend inside and all around me.

"About ten years ago, I went to a memorial service for a deceased lawyer. I had not known him well, but as I sat in the service with open eyes, a vision of him came to me. He told me that everything was wonderful, that the place he was in made him very happy. The entire background of the whole vision was white and he had an immaculate smile. After that, I had several visions of and talks with other deceased lawyers. I believe that my Higher Self was letting me know that death was safe.

"When I was in the process of divorce about four years ago, I began having dreams that were very powerful, both while I was awake and asleep! For instance, one night I dreamed that I was choking and the next night I dreamed that I heard someone knocking at my door. This dream seemed so real that I actually went to the door and opened only to find no one there. I tore off my shirt, thinking this would stop the choking. When I consulted a dream therapist, I came to understand that my Higher Self was telling me to 'open up and not choke my unconscious mind.'

"There was a great void in my life at this time. I had been married for twenty years and did not want the divorce at first. I was so depressed that I literally sat in a corner for three whole days and nights, reading and praying. I believe that what I felt must be akin to what someone contemplating suicide might feel. Finally, an inner voice seemed to speak to me, 'You have a choice: sit here or get up!' With great effort, I arose and it suddenly began raining. I felt God was cleansing me and that I was starting afresh. I went ahead with the divorce and have remained friendly with my former wife.

"At two different seminars, I looked into someone's eyes and saw God! On another occasion, I experienced that, although I had been taught intolerance and racial prejudice as a child, I felt unconditional love for many of the people present. The feelings of prejudice had melted away! Later that same year, I visited Russia and, again, that sense of love and understanding flooded my awareness. I experienced the people as kind, understanding and friendly. My earlier judgments about the 'awful Russian Communists' had disappeared.

"During a rebirthing session, a difficult problem with my mother was resolved. She had been critical, saying many hurtful things to me. I suddenly felt I was lying in a canoe moving down a stream when I saw an island which I then realized was the placenta. I was in the womb! Then I was being born and she smiled at me and asked the doctors if everything was okay. They said I was perfect. My mother's smile healed me and I have had a better relationship with her ever since.

"On a day-to-day basis, I feel peaceful and happy. As long as I remain in touch with my Higher Self, my life is steady and even. Before I get out of bed in the morning, I ask God to be with me and everyone I come into contact with throughout the day. I find, then, that most problems just fall into place. I have even experienced having eight or ten cases set for court simultaneously with no idea how they would work out. But they always somehow become resolved when I remain in touch with my Higher Self. This inner power instructs and helps me to send out love to everyone around me and I feel it radiating back around to me."

Paul: Experience in Joy

"June 2, 1987: Today it occurred to me that (all my life) I have felt that there was nothing of value in me. Everything of importance was outside of me, even God. Last night Christina rebirthed me. I saw inside myself and it was all goodness and light and joy! It was the very first time in my life that I remember experiencing joy! It was as if there was a shaft of light inside of me. I felt totally connected to myself, my higher power and that light."

"June 18, 1987: Since the first of June I have been rebirthed four times and in those rebirths I have gotten more in touch with the divine and the spirit within me than in all the Masses and church services I have ever attended."

Margie Sees A Being of Light

"I had unconsciously blamed myself for my little brother's death. He was four and I was eight and I was supposed to take care of him. He had spinal meningitis but I still thought it was my fault. The other night I was meditating and suddenly someone was there, saying to me, 'You blame yourself for Jimmy's death, but it wasn't your fault, Margie.' Then a white light appeared and it became a beautiful golden light, a figure of a being, neither male nor female, but both. It came close to me. It was surrounded by pink light. It felt wonderful, peaceful, powerful! I asked the being who it was but it didn't answer. I didn't move closer to it because I didn't want it to leave. I don't know who it was."

When I told Margie that the "Being" was her Higher Self, she burst into tears, immediately, joyfully recognizing that this was true. Our Higher Self is so exalted, so radiantly pure, that when we first experience this encounter, we think it is someone else. We have no idea that a part of us is so exalted!

Michelle

"When my brother-in-law developed cancer, I immediately began to pray for his recovery. I used every opportunity for prayer, even turning off the car radio to use silent driving time to communicate with God. Within a few days, my husband was also hospitalized, succumbing to stress he was experiencing because of his brother's illness.

"As I prayed at home alone one night, asking for understanding, wondering why I seemed to be so calm amidst all the upheaval, I suddenly felt a Holy Presence in the bedroom with me. The Presence spoke to me clearly, telling me that I was calm because, for the first time in my life, I had totally relinquished a problem to the care of the Divine with complete faith that God does hear and answer our prayers. At that moment, I knew without question that I was in the presence of the Living God, which I experience with awe and a feeling of great honor, humbled that it could happen to me!

"I have experienced this connection since, usually in connection to intercessory prayers for others. I have been given expanded knowledge during these experiences, as well as a few surprising 'assignments,' involving healing, forgiveness, release from fear of death, addiction issues and how our prayers intercede for others.

"These experiences may seem empty, lifeless or 'unreal' when related verbally. In truth, these holy moments are more vibrant and real than any life experiences I have ever had. It seems like these moments are the real ones and that day-to-day living is the illusion!"

Ingrid: Spiritual Awakening

"I was not on any spiritual journey but I knew something was missing in my life. Nothing seemed to make sense. My lover left me for someone else; it was a totally devastating experience. I felt abandoned, betrayed, cheated and totally worthless. I felt like I had a big hole in my chest — like there was nothing for me to hold onto. I was in so much pain it was all I could do to get from one hour to the next.

"I especially remember one morning a few days after it happened. I had spent the night before with friends and felt I couldn't express my real feelings at their house and had held a lot of pain inside. The next morning I went home and just fell apart. It was so bad. I have never felt so horrible in my life. I contemplated suicide. It was just unbearably painful. I began crying but it was not just crying — it was more like howling like an animal. There was just nothing left for me. I felt total despair.

"This went on for a while and suddenly from deep inside I heard/felt a voice that said, "I am here." At first I felt bewildered because I didn't know who it was. But I felt comforted. Also I began to feel that my father (long deceased) was with me. It felt like he was holding my right hand.

"Before that time I had no spiritual orientation of any kind. I was just floundering. And now it just felt so wonderful to feel the comfort coming from inside! After that morning there were moments when I doubted my sanity . . . but I didn't care because it just felt so reassuring to have this inner comfort! This experience was really the start of my spiritual journey because I realized there was more than I ever thought there was. I realized I could connect directly to God. This was the beginning of my spiritual awakening. This inner voice has been with me ever since. I still feel depressed or upset at times, but it is never the total emptiness I used to experience because deep inside me now I know I am not alone."

Although she did not realize what was happening at the time, Ingrid was clearing her inner channel by allowing herself to feel "all that unbearable pain," which was suppressed negative energy in the form of fears of abandonment and other very old emotions, most likely stored since birth and early childhood. That clearing allowed her Higher Self to make the contact with her conscious mind which she describes in this story. Although her Higher Self was always there, waiting, it was not until the inner channel was sufficiently cleared that she was able to perceive its comforting presence. Ingrid's experience illustrates so beautifully that the Higher Self has its own perfect timing whether we have any idea that we are growing or not. She was not "on a path" or making any conscious effort to grow spiritually — yet when it was time for her to break through to the conscious connection with her Higher Self, it happened spontaneously.

Kirsten: Transformation of Fear

"During a connected breathing session, in my inward experience I suddenly was back in Europe, when I was 3 or 4 years old. I was standing on the beach wearing a blue dress. My mother and a man were there. It was very dark and as I looked out toward the Ocean, I saw a huge black wave coming right at me. I was afraid it was going to engulf me and I felt completely helpless to stop it. My mother did not seem to be aware that I was in any danger; she was not paying attention to me at that particular moment."

"I now believe that when I was about that age, I was overpowered by emotions so intense I felt they were drowning me. Subsequently, throughout my life I have felt I had to strongly control emotions. This inner experience cleared it up, though, for since then I am much less afraid of powerful emotions. Now they just feel like a natural, healthy way to release intense energy."

While it is not appropriate to assign universal meanings to any person's inward images, water frequently seems to represent emotions. Certainly this would apply here, since the explanation given above is Kirsten's own intuitive understanding.

She notes that the beach experience ended at the moment she (a) felt the fear that the wave was going to engulf her, (b) felt helpless to stop it and (c) felt the aloneness because her mother was not aware that she was in danger. Apparently, the combination of these powerful emotions was so frightening to the tiny girl that she had suppressed them into unconsciousness. *Experiencing them in a fully conscious state (during the rebirth) thus allowed their integration into her expanding wholeness and she, therefore, is now more comfortable with intense emotions. That separate cell of fear in the subconscious having been opened and its energy absorbed, there is no longer any unconscious, energy-charged substance for fear to "hook into!"*

Whether or not the beach experience ever actually occurred in the outer, physical dimension is immaterial. The important factor is that Kirsten's unconscious mind effectively utilized this scenario to bring about her healing.

Kirsten adds: "A while after I began rebirthing, I went to a political meeting and to my astonishment, when it came my turn to stand up in front of a whole roomful of people, I was able to speak with no panic, whereas before I couldn't even speak in front of a few friends. Also, my experiences have confirmed for me that I have been doing what I was meant to do in this life. I have a greater feeling of peace within myself now and I am more at peace with others. I listen to the inner voice more and doubt it less, trusting that its guidance is right for me.

"Another remarkable result is the experience of being one with the power of God, the spirit presence, and the feeling of absolute joy and love and wonderment, which I have experienced since I started rebirthing! Before, I was aware of an inner spirit but it seemed like it was at a distance; since rebirthing, it's more of an immediate contact, always very close."

Lisa Meets Her Unborn Child

"I was pregnant and, although I wanted a child very much, I did not want to marry the father of the child. I made the decision to have an abortion and then felt terribly sad and guilty afterward.

"Several years later I met a man I really loved and we were married. We wanted a child, but after more than a year of marriage, I still had not conceived. It was then that I discovered connected breathing. After breathing for just a few minutes, I began to feel the enormous sadness over the aborted child. Christina breathed with me, encouraging me to allow myself to let all those feelings come up. I kept breathing and got through it.

"Suddenly I felt like I was in a tunnel-like place moving toward an opening ahead. It was warm there and full of love and I knew that I was in the womb. I was screaming out at first and it felt like I was ridding myself of some fears I had while in the womb. Once past this stage, I went on to an even warmer, more loving space.

"From the left side came a sparkling sphere of light, full of energy, which I recognized as my child which had been aborted. I cried and told this child that I was sorry; I asked it to forgive me and to come back to me. I felt great love coming from this child and felt that I was forgiven. Then I asked God to forgive me, too. That felt so good; I felt clean like a newborn! Then I was able to forgive myself!

"Then from in front of me came a second sphere of light — the child who would be born in the future as my son and I called him by name. I told both of them how much we love and want them. I felt overwhelmed by the love of these children.

"The old, unfinished business was now complete and I felt entirely ready to conceive a child. A few months later, I did become pregnant and our beautiful, healthy son came into our lives!"

It was very important for Lisa to verbally express her love to the aborted child and specifically ask for its forgiveness. In relating with that child, she was relating with a part of herself. Although she loved the child and had felt sorry all along about the abortion, it was not until she actively obtained forgiveness and expressed that love that this energy integrated into her conscious awareness.

Carol: Merging into Oneness

"The most expansive experiences of my life have occurred in the presence of other people. The synergy of the collective energies seems to help me transcend ordinary consciousness.

"In my work as a psychotherapist, I sometimes utilize non-traditional techniques such as guided imagery. Recently I was guiding a client through such a meditation in order to help her make connection with her inner child, that real self inside each of us. Directing her to close her eyes, I closed mine, too, as I took her through a process to help her relax even more deeply. Slowly I led her in fantasy into a beautiful forest, then along a wooded path and through a green meadow, where she saw and connected with her inner child.

"After about five minutes, I noticed that my hands, which were lying palms up on my lap, were tingling and seemed to overflow with energy. I could not feel the boundaries of my fingers; they seemed to merge with the space around them. My hands felt huge! I felt total peace and oneness with the Universe and realized that divine energy was flowing through me to heal my client.

"I remember wondering how I could ever doubt my connection with the Higher Power. I was intensely aware that we are all indeed one, always loved and protected!"

Like Carol, I have noticed that some of the most powerful experiences in my life have occurred when I was intensely focused on someone or something else. No doubt the absence of self-consciousness is an important component in moving beyond the familiar ego boundaries in the mind.

Namaste'

In India it is customary to greet others by pressing one's palms together, bowing the head slightly and saying, "Namaste," (nah' mah stay), a Sanskrit word which means, "I bow to the God in you!" Once you have had the experience of opening to your Higher Self, you will understand how this lovely custom probably originated. It is a dignified expression of reverence and respect for another person, and a reminder each time it is used that each of us is essentially divine. It is my joy to share it with you; it is a wonderful addition to one's vocabulary.

If you are really sincere in your quest for higher consciousness, you will be guided to a meeting with your Higher Self at the perfect time. There need be no hurry, unless you are impatient with evolution at a snail's pace, as I was. In that case, there are safe, reliable and effective ways to speed up the process. In other chapters, I have written about Connected Breathing and (especially) Meditation, which are safe, direct ways to greatly speed up your evolution.

Inner Receptivity Determines Your Growth

It is helpful to remember that it is not the addition of something from outside that brings the joy and serenity of higher consciousness to your life; it is your inner receptivity that determines how much and how quickly you can attune to the higher vibrations. You can go to collect water from the ocean with a thimble or a bucket; what you receive is determined by the size of the container, not by the ocean itself. The techniques given in this book are very fast ways to clear the inner channels of your receptivity, opening the way for omnipresent light and love to energize and transform your life.

Exercise to Begin Opening to Your Higher Self:

Sit comfortably or lie down and take a few deep breaths, relaxing completely from head to toe. With every breath, feel that you are relaxing more deeply. Use the visualization of the rainbow colors, red, orange, yellow, green, blue, purple, violet and white, to enter a deeper state of awareness. Now imagine that in the space right above you, there is a shaft of soft, radiant white light. Feel now that you welcome the awareness that the light is always there above you, guiding and directing your life. Stay in this restful, peaceful space for as long as you like, then come back to an ordinary waking state whenever you wish, knowing that from now on the light will over-shadow you.

Affirmation:

"I now surrender to the guidance and direction of my Higher Self."

11

Personal Law

"As a man thinketh in his heart, so is he."
Proverbs 23:7

The energy of the Universe functions like a giant affirmation machine — no matter what we believe, it is as though life holds up a big sign saying, "That's right! You're right!" So let's discuss why this is true and how it works.

The very purpose of life is for you to finally realize your own true identity as a child of God; you are a divine being creating your own experience of life.

Your thoughts when combined with your feelings are creating your world, 100% of it! But it doesn't seem like that is true, does it? It often seems more like you are a victim of circumstances trying to figure out the rules of a complex game.

We are divine beings, children of God, part of the Creator, but most of us have to hear this message many times and from many different sources before we begin to really absorb the message that it is literally true that we are divine beings, heirs to all the wealth of the Universe! It is because we are divine that our thoughts are always creative. Whether we remember who we are or not, we are creating our experience, our drama, our lives. If we direct our thoughts and feelings positively, we create positive, happy, wonderful experiences.   If, however, we use our free will to set up a negative drama, we are still just as creative and will experience unhappy, fearful, ugly experiences in life.

Like a person with amnesia, we have forgotten who we are. We think the circumstances in our lives, the drama all around us, is happening to us! We have forgotten that we are divine creators and that we are creating all this ourselves with our thoughts and feelings!

So how does the Universe wake you up to remember who you truly are? What can wake you up to realize how all this is being created — that it is you who are creating it in the first place? By having the Universal law or principle operate very consistently. Whatever you think about and have strong feelings about, will manifest in your life experience! You can begin to observe this in your own life.

Most people have one or more very negative beliefs, usually unconscious, which contaminates their life experience. Rebirthers often call such a negative belief one's "Personal Law." It is very important to discover your Personal Law because as long as it remains unconscious, it will be very powerful in your life, attracting a negative pattern of experiences. Once you determine what your negative Personal Law is, you can begin to bring it more into your conscious awareness, practice conscious choice when you see the thought affecting your life and use the techniques in this book to change it.

At least half of all people have a negative Personal Law that is some variation of "I'm not good enough." A good rebirther or other loving, conscious professional can assist you in discovering any negative, self-sabotaging thought which may be causing an undercurrent of difficulty in your life.

Examples of Personal Laws:

Here are some examples of Personal Laws and possible circumstances which could lead to such negative conclusions.

1. "I'm not enough" or "I'm not good enough" or some variation on this theme.

This conclusion could be drawn for a great many reasons, which explains why at least half of the population is burdened with this one. It could be because your parents wanted a boy and you are a girl or vice versa. Or they were already unhappy with themselves and looked to their new baby to make them happy (which, of course, you were unable to do!) and so you concluded, "I'm not good enough!"

2. "My aliveness hurts people!" If your mother experienced a lot of pain during labor, you may have decided that it was your fault and unconsciously believe, "My aliveness hurts people." With such a Personal Law, one would tend to hold back, be passive and avoid spontaneity. Counteract it with a positive affirmation like: "Everybody is happy because I am alive!"

3. "I don't belong here." If your parents did not want a child at all or if they wanted a child of a different gender than you are, then you could have concluded, "I don't belong here." (People with this Personal Law usually have difficulty finding their niche and tend to move a lot.) A good affirmation might be: "I always belong wherever I am."

4. "Intimacy is dangerous." People who were handled roughly as an infant sometimes conclude that they will be safer if they don't allow anyone to get too close to them. This Personal Law might express itself as, "Intimacy is dangerous; I can't allow anyone to get too close!" This person might have many superficial

relationships but not be truly intimate with anyone! Affirmation: "The more true intimacy I experience, the safer I am!"

5. "People abandon me." or sometimes, "Women abandon me." An individual who did not receive sufficient touching and nurturing care as an infant may have felt abandoned. Note that this is not necessarily a negative comment on the parent or other caretaker. Some babies need more attention than others. But if the infant felt abandoned, then that abandonment is a real issue for him, regardless of the care he may have received. Also, it is believed that babies delivered by Caeserean section sometimes have abandonment issues because they had to "abandon the womb," i.e., they did not have the natural experience of moving through the birth canal. The person affected in any of these ways might have an unconscious thought that "people abandon me." This belief gets turned around into an unconscious command like, "Abandon me!" or the person may cling so much out of the fear of abandonment that, although a loved one might wish to stay, he is actually driven away by the clinging. Thus, the very fear of abandonment will have directly created the abandonment! Begin to change this negative thought with an affirmation like: "People love to be in my presence" or "I am always safe and happy, whether I am alone or with others."

One more comment on Caeserean babies: because the birth process is interrupted and they are "lifted out" and do not have to push through the birth canal as in the natural birth process, these people sometimes will expect to be helped out or rescued after what may seem like just a little bit of effort on their part. Be aware that this will seem utterly natural to them although others around them may not experience it that way.

6. "There is not enough for me!" The ideal nutrition for a newborn baby is mother's milk. Not only does baby get a perfect formula, but he gets it from his own mother, in whose very body he has been formed. He gets held by her, he takes in her smell, she gazes on him lovingly, he hears the reassuring sound of her heartbeat which he has been used to hearing all through his life in the womb. For a newborn, this is everything in the world he wants or needs! If, however, he was breastfed but only on a schedule, he may have spent periods of time feeling hungry before feeding time. Or if baby was bottle fed, the formula may not have agreed with his little system and he may have felt frustrated and very hungry. These and other infantile experiences can lead to a conclusion that "There is not enough for me." And then that person may unconsciously create circumstances where there is not enough or it may not arrive soon enough to feel comfortable. Many times financial shortages seem to be directly linked to how one was fed as a baby. If any of these situations seem to fit in your experience, try working with an affirmation like,"There is always enough of everything for me at just the time I need it!"

These few examples will give you some idea of how the thoughts and beliefs we accept as infants can affect our life experiences. I encourage you to discover any negative thought(s) which may be obstructing your progress for you can then use the techniques in this book to make wonderful changes in your life. It may help to re-read the section on Affirmations. Give these concepts and techniques a real test in your life before you make any decision about them.

12

Experiencing Your Feelings

"Your health is bound to be affected if, day after day, you say the opposite of what you feel, if you grovel before what you dislike and rejoice at what brings you nothing but misfortune."
                                    Dr. Zhivago

Loving yourself includes accepting without judgment all your feelings, including fear, anxiety, sadness, anger and guilt. It includes accepting both your emotions and the feelings in your body. It even includes accepting your judgmental thoughts about yourself and others. Connecting your breath while all those feelings are occurring will allow you to fully experience them without "shutting down" or suppressing any of them. And then they will become integrated into your expanded awareness.

Whenever you experience negative energy, one of two things will happen: (1) You can choose to begin connecting your breaths and welcome the feelings, no matter how uncomfortable or (2) you will suppress the energy, store it and carry it around on an unconscious level where it will create more negative experiences in your life. Like attracts like.

The next time you experience negative energy, try this: Begin breathing and remind yourself that this is an opportunity to breathe through it, feel it all and accept it as a rejected part of yourself which you have separated off. This will allow it to integrate. When it integrates, it will feel as though it has been released because it will no longer have power as a separate cell of energy.

Integrating the unaccepted, rejected parts of yourself will free your energy from suppressions. You will then begin feeling the beautiful, loving, happy feelings which are present in all people and which are felt when the channel is clear enough of suppression. And beyond these emotions, you will feel the space of bliss or joyfulness which is the absence of all emotions.

Acting out negative emotions (i.e., steaming off at the other driver in traffic, snapping at your child when your upset is over something that occurred at the office, blaming anything 'out there' for your woes), does not cause them to integrate; if anything, it fuels the fire only, leaving you feeling less than good about your behavior. "Owning" your feelings (I am feeling very angry right now - I have a lot of anger inside) without blaming them on anyone else, and allowing yourself to feel them, will effectively integrate the energy. (Note that it is important not to blame yourself, either! Just claim ownership of the energy that is being felt as anger right at the moment.) When you experience this process even once, you will never forget it; it feels like a miracle has occurred, because you usually move (very quickly) from feeling just awful to feeling really happy and clear, as though you have had a psychic and emotional bath. You will be experiencing the power and magic of the present moment!

When an orange is squeezed it emits orange juice, because that is what is inside an orange! When you are "squeezed" in some way, whatever comes out of you is whatever was inside in the first place. It is a mistake to blame the person or situation that squeezed you. If you are full of love, you will respond lovingly, even to a negative situation. If you have a lot of suppressed anger, you will react angrily, regardless of the degree of provocation. And often you will actually create or attract a situation that will let you feel the anger so you will have the opportunity to deal with it. If it is your experience that one upsetting circumstance after another crops up in your life, you may want to confer with a Rebirther to help get in touch with suppressed anger.

Suppressions Block Life Force

The Universal life force energy cannot move through you if you have suppressions. It wants to support you to be whole and happy and, therefore, sends ample opportunities for you to get clear of the suppressions. So you can see that suppressing anger is really like placing an order for something to come up in your life that will anger you!

Many people have grown up believing that anger, sadness and other negative emotions are bad. Actually, feelings are neither good nor bad; they just are. There is no such thing as negative or positive energy; there is only energy. But we use our conscious minds to label and judge as either negative or positive based on what we like or dislike.

When we feel a negative feeling and do not allow ourselves to experience it fully, because of our judgment that it is somehow unacceptable, we suppress (store) it. It then becomes subconscious where it is most powerful. Suppressed negative energy is responsible for creating most of the unpleasant circumstances in our lives.

Holding in suppressed anger leads to depression. Next time you feel depressed, ask yourself, "What am I angry about?" Just admitting to yourself that you are angry will be a start in the direction of lifting the depression.

The following exercise is very effective and healing when you get into reaction (feel "hooked" by a negative feeling). There was a time in my life when I copied it in block letters onto a 3x5 card and kept it on my refrigerator, to remind myself to use it at that critical moment when I would feel "hooked":

1. Breathe (Connected breaths - no pauses).

2. Recognize the reaction and own it.
   Identify it. What emotion are you feeling?

3. Feel it. Let yourself feel it. Get in touch with it. How big is it? What color is it? Where in your body is it located? Does it feel heavy? Solid? What else?

4. Tell the truth about it (at least to yourself).
   No games; no manipulating or blaming anyone else. What old pattern are you running here?

5. Have compassion for yourself. Forgive yourself.

6. Experience that it is safe to be vulnerable, to feel these feelings now.

7. Choose love for yourself.

13

Becoming Whole

Holiness is also spelled "wholeness."

In the quest for wholeness, paradox is at every turn. It is so true that we cannot realize our wholeness as long as we deny any fragment of ourselves. If we seek to avoid fear or pain or sadness, we will simultaneously block the love and joy and laughter from our awareness. That pain, fear or sadness contains great stores of energy, which can be released for potent creative and constructive use only after it is consciously felt and thus allowed to integrate. A truly healthy person, one who has power over himself and his own life, is courageous enough to become willing to experience whatever life has in store.

Some of the personal experiences recounted in this book provide excellent examples of an individual reaching the "gold" inside because he had struggled through the "muck!" During the orientation process with a new rebirthing client, I sometimes compare the breath to a drill boring through the granite of a mountain. If one has no faith that there really is gold in that mountain, he may give up after one attempt; he may even go away thinking to himself that "there is nothing to connected breathing!" This attitude usually indicates that that person just isn't ready to begin accelerated healing and growth work. And that is okay, for indeed it may be better to coast a while longer rather than to take off on a new track before being fully ready to go. When a person adopts this attitude, there is little I or anyone else can (or should) do but perhaps realize that this individual is not ready yet, or that he chooses to delay his discovery of the gold in the mountain until some other time.   When you are truly ready to begin your growth process and glimpse that there is gold in the mountain, however, you will not become discouraged because you do not strike the rich vein immediately. You will not give up after a few brief, restless meditation periods; you will not quit after one rebirthing experience. After all, the richest treasure of all, the inner gold, is not that easily won!

The little self in all of us prefers to be lazy, to keep doing things the way we've always done them. It wants to shirk responsibility and blame someone or something else for every shortcoming. It wants the gold, for sure, but wants it handed over without much effort. But this gold of self realization can only be gained by one willing to plunge into his own mountain, willing to keep drilling into the solid rock, willing to grope through the dark, dank caves filled with terrors lurking in the shadows, by one who refuses to stop short of reconnection with the pure gold of his Higher Self. Comparing the unknown, fearful elements hiding in one's consciousness to monsters lurking in a dark cave is an appropriate metaphor. Indeed, it may require even more courage to face the inner monsters.It is encouraging to realize that this process of piercing through the last obstacles comes when you are nearing the end of your journey. The loving, skilled support of a conscious, competent rebirther can help you move safely through these fearful spaces when, alone, you might give up the effort.

The whole purpose of repeated lifetimes on Earth is finally to remember your true identity as a perfect child of God. To the extent that in your mountain there is solid rock of rigid false beliefs that you have not drilled into and dislodged, to the extent that there are monsters of fear slithering in the dark shadows of hidden caves, to that extent you have forgotten who you are. When you are ready, you will bore through the granite and head toward those monsters. As soon as you face them, the cave becomes illuminated. And you will see that this "haunted house," so scary in the darkness, was just illusion all along. But for as long as you cringe in fear, for as long as your little self can frighten you into staying away from the light switch on the wall beyond the monsters, for that long will the terrible darkness persist.

In Jungian terms, this process of facing the monsters within would be called "owning your own shadow," the shadow being all those qualities you have chosen to disown and, subsequently, to "make wrong" and judge, whether you inherited those judgments from your family, religion and culture or chose them all by yourself. The critical element is to "own" them; they are, after all is said and done, all yours! When you get through all the infantile kicking and screaming and playing the victim, when you get through your anger that "they did it to you," these obstacles will still be there waiting for you, for they can be faced and uprooted by no one else. "Owning" this responsibility for having created your own life just as it is, can be scary indeed, for the very next stage is usually anger at oneself for having chosen these present circumstances and, ultimately, we fear our own anger and self-judgment most of all. But it is not constructive to dawdle at that stage, wallowing in rage and self-pity. It works much better to love yourself and forgive yourself. Practice saying aloud, "I forgive myself for _____," no matter how unforgiveable you may think it is! (We all have our "unforgiveables!") Say these words even if it doesn't feel like you mean them at first.

Blame is meaningless; it never serves anyone. It is as much a delusion to begin blaming yourself as to blame someone else.The Universe has no desire to punish you; it just wants you to wake up! All that is important is to get through any barrier to your Higher Self. The direct route is to realize that, as a Spirit Being, you always choose your experiences. You will discover that when you stop pointing a finger at anyone else, when you stop assigning any of the responsibility to anything else, then you are finally beginning to shake off your amnesia and remember who you are: a Being of Light, a Spirit Being who creates his own life. Then you will cower no longer in feigned helplessness; you will simply begin creating anew. You will have turned on the Light!

Dr. Bob Samples in The Metaphoric Mind, offers a fascinating example of wholeness. He assigns the three human expressions of physical/sexual, emotional and intellectual each to one of the ridges of a three-sided pyramid, pointing out that most people in any culture focus on developing and expressing only one ridge, neglecting to some extent the development of the remaining two human attributes. For example, a businessman might use his intellect almost exclusively, with little emotional development and may also neglect health and expression through his physical body. An athlete might focus almost entirely on physical body development, somewhat to the exclusion of his intellectual or emotional life. And the remaining imbalance could be found in the emotional person who does not develop his intellectual or physical expressions.

In the more highly-developed person, two of the three ridges are developed in greater balance. An example of this would be a dancer, who focuses and expresses life force energy in both the physical/sexual and emotional areas. Society grants implied permission to males to be predominately intellectual, to a lesser extent physical/sexual, but not emotional. Women are expected to be emotional and to a lesser degree physical/sexual, but not intellectual. The third duo is reserved for the celibate cleric: that person is expected to express intellectually, to a lesser extent emotionally, but suppress physical/sexual expression! And, of course, all of these polarizations are entirely arbitrary. They are a fragmenting of the human person, requiring him to shut down great portions of his human expression in exchange for acceptance by family, culture and society. Most people make the trade; the pain of isolation and rejection by others is usually too great a price to pay, even for full personhood.

Rules of culture and society tend to polarize us into remaining near the base of the pyramid where each of the three functions is distant from the others. There comes a time, though, when one is content only with realization and expression of all the areas of himself - physical, intellectual and emotional. As that person begins to develop himself more fully, he begins ascending the pyramid. Moving up to expressing two of the elements greatly augments the energy directed into the life, resulting in feelings of involvement, well-being and self-worth. Functioning in a balanced way with all three qualities of body, mind and emotions leads to the pyramid's summit, which is the experience of wholeness or spirituality. Society calls this genius.

In your wholeness, you are a powerful, unlimited being. But you can only find that out by allowing in the Light. Using the techniques in this book to turn the spotlight inward and begin the process of illumination will speed you quickly along. Forget about the faults of others; ignore the things that are wrong with the world. If you want to render real service, begin your own illumination process. This will do more to heal the world than a thousand years of identifying what is wrong!

14

The Magic of Surrender

*"I am a child of the Universe and I am willing
to experience whatever the Universe has in
store for me."*
               Carol W. Parrish

It was 1977. My toddler and I were leaving on a
midnight train for Chicago. Already awake for 18 hours
I felt fairly exhausted; my daughter, however, gave all
indications of easily having another 18 hours of reserve
energy. Arriving at the station, feeling almost punchy
with fatigue, I held onto the thought that soon I could
collapse in a sleeping compartment beside this 20-
month-old dynamo! My father, so proud of his young
granddaughter, accompanied us to the ticket counter,
carrying her as he had carried me when I was a baby.

The young ticket agent checked the computer,
turned to me and apologetically advised, "There must
be some mistake, ma'am; there is no sleeping compartment available for you." "But how can that be?" I asked,
"I reconfirmed our reservations just this afternoon!"
"I'm sorry," he responded, "it must be a computer error.
This train is booked almost to capacity. I can give you
a coach seat, but you will most likely have to hold your
baby in your lap!" With the exhaustion I already felt,
just the thought of sitting up all night in a crowded
coach, holding my sleeping little one seemed overwhelming at that moment. I could feel anger begin to
rise from my toes!

After a few enraged seconds, an angry scene on its way, I glanced at my father, so in love with his precious grandchild, and thought to myself, "No matter how angry I feel, I will not ruin our last few minutes together! I love him and us too much for that." I then interiorized my consciousness briefly and prayed my prayer of surrender, "Beloved God, if I have to sit up all night long and hold this baby, I will do it sweetly, with your help. I will be a channel for love in that coach full of people!" Instantly all anger left me and I felt peace and poise return. Tears welled up in my eyes as I suddenly felt a blissful divine presence all around me.

Everything seemed so different than it had just moments before. All it took to make this difficult situation easy was to surrender to it and remember that my only purpose here is to love. I felt enveloped in an aura of divine love as we turned and proceeded together to the train platform outside.

We stood watching the approaching headlights of the powerful locomotive booming toward us, my father lovingly holding onto our last few minutes together and I intoxicated with the joy that continued to permeate my awareness. Suddenly I heard someone from inside the station running toward us, calling my name. It was the young ticket agent. Breathless, he reached us and blurted out: "I don't understand this at all, Mrs. Thomas. We don't have the compartment you reserved, but we have one twice as large that you can have for the price of the smaller one!" What joy and gratitude flooded my being! Not only for the sleeping compartment, but for the miracle I was experiencing! Boarding the train with tears in my eyes, I no longer felt any awareness of exhaustion. Love, alone, was my experience now.

Years later when she was about eight years old, my daughter was wrestling with a difficult situation at school. It seemed to call for surrender and I told her this story. She asked, ". . . so does this mean that if I am willing to give up what I want, I'll get twice as much?" "No," I responded, "I don't think we can make deals like that with God. We have to be prepared to give up what we think we want rather than giving up peace and love, and then sometimes we also receive more of what we wanted."

15

The Power of Commitment

*"Whatever you do may seem insignificant
but it is very important that you do it."*
Mahatma Gandhi

Commitment is the way to engage all of your energy in one direction. Like using a laser beam instead of a BB Gun, the intense focus of your intention in a single direction is very powerful.

Commitment is either 100% or it is zero! There is no such thing as a 99% commitment; 99% = zero! Just like a strong chain with one weak link, a 99% commitment will break when the uncommitted 1% is challenged. A less-than-100% commitment is really just an agreement or understanding, whether unilateral or bilateral, that you will behave in certain prescribed ways. It may work for convenience but it will not energize your life!

Commitment aligns your energy, creating a force more powerful than any obstacle that can come your way. It is not imprisoning, but liberating. In a personal relationship, for instance, a real commitment frees both partners from any concern about other people. The commitment actually allows each partner to relate to others in a relaxed fashion, for the parties already know what their behavior is going to be. Therefore, the question of infidelity never arises. Until you are sure that you want to be in a relationship, it is better not to make a commitment. However, at such time as you are ready to move the relationship to a higher level, a total commitment will be necessary.

Living within a committed relationship will require you to reach for your highest potential like few other circumstances in life. If you wish to truly grow, you may very well achieve that growth by finding a partner with whom you can be totally committed, who feels the same way about you and about his or her goals.

Commitment is Essential to Happiness

If you find that a personal relationship is not appropriate (or not available) temporarily or permanently, you can continue to live and develop your potential very powerfully by finding a cause or mission to which you personally can feel very dedicated, and form your committed relationship with that dedication. But you cannot be happy without commitment!

In order to fully engage your life force energy, which is the essence of you, you need a commitment. Without a commitment, your energy will not flow in a given direction. It will scatter around one experience or another, but you won't have much sense of accomplishment because you never were clear about your mission! You see, it is not important whether a cause needs you. What is important is that you need a cause!

Any cause will work, as long as you are fully congruent in your desire and dedication to it. Your cause may be grand and global or it may be your own private mission. You may choose to let the world know about it, or you may choose to keep it your ultimate secret! But whatever it is, to be effective as a tool for energizing your life, you must be 100% committed to it.

Commitment exists when you are willing to do whatever it takes to serve the cause or mission to which you are committed.

Until one is committed there is hesitancy
the chance to draw back, always ineffectiveness.

Concerning all acts of initiative (and creation),
there is one elementary truth, the ignorance of
which kills countless ideas and splendid dreams:
that the moment one definitely commits oneself,
then Providence moves, too.

All sorts of things occur to help one that would
never otherwise have occurred.

A whole stream of events issues from the decision
raising in one's favor all manner of unforeseen
incidents and meetings and material assistance,
which no man could have dreamed would have
come his way.

"Are you in earnest? Seize this very minute:
What you can do, or dream you can, begin it;
Boldness has genius, power and magic in it.
Only engage and then the mind grows heated;
Begin and then the work will be completed."
                           Goethe

16

Doing What You Love to Do

" Where Love is, God is."   Leo Tolstoy

When you are doing what you love to do, you feel joy, happiness and a connection to life itself. At the energy level, you become a wide-open channel and the life force of the Universe flows through you freely, bringing an intense aliveness to whatever you are doing, to the place where you are and to everyone in the vicinity of your consciousness. You actually let go of the awareness of yourself as a separate being as you become part of a greater consciousness.

This "losing yourself" in a greater wholeness than your little separate self is really only a losing of the sense of separateness itself. (The limited conscious mind - ego - would rather be separate than happy!) So nothing of value is lost; in fact, everything worthwhile is gained.

This is what Jesus meant when he said, "He who loseth his life for my sake shall find it." (Matthew 10:30). That is, he who surrenders his separate ego identity for the greater identity as an indivisible part of the perfection and wholeness of the Universe shall find his own true life.

Functioning at this level of consciousness, in tune with the Universal flow, you automatically make choices and decisions that work perfectly without input from your rational, logical mind. Whatever you need to know, do, be or have will become available just at the time needed. Jesus was again referring to this state when he advised: " ... take no thought how or what ye shall speak, for it shall be given you in that same hour what ye shall speak." (Matthew 10:19). Meaning: "Do not use your little conscious ego mind to figure out what you are going to say, (but stay in that consciousness where you are part of the oneness with the Universal energy) and you will know what to say when it is time to speak."

You will recognize this state of consciousness by a feeling of comfort in your body, a feeling of being in your place, of happiness, lightness and a lack of self-consciousness.

There is an old story about a miller and his wife who lived in a small village in Europe. They spent their days grinding wheat into flour and making it into bread to supply their entire village. They loved each other very much and expressed their love joyfully as they worked together making their bread. The energy of their love permeated every loaf of bread without their even thinking about it. The people of the village consumed the bread and were energized and blessed with the vibration of love in the bread.

In like fashion, when you work at something you love to do, the very power and force of your love blesses not only you, but everyone and everything around you. Doing what you love to do is a potent way to love yourself and attune to Universal Life Force Energy. It is the way to be happy and successful in a flowing, effortless way.

For most of our history, people have assumed that they must work at something in order to make money, with little or no regard for how they felt about that work.

When you hold onto a job which you do not enjoy, you naturally resent it, resenting the time spent on the job, dreading the thought of getting up in the morning to go to work, and not even enjoying the time off work because of the dread of going back to work again. You feel no joy in what you are doing and you may become unpleasant to be around. The flow of Universal Life Force Energy is blocked. In this way you are expressing a belief that the Universe is an unfriendly place, a place of scarcity, not a place of abundance that will support you unconditionally and perfectly.

Working like this is actually a disservice to yourself and everyone else on the planet. Your highest purpose here is to love and keep yourself open to the joy that will pour through you unless you do something to block it. Everyone will be blessed if you are in a state of joyfulness. Your happiness is thus a direct service to mankind.

You may not even know what it is you love to do. (This would be an example of not loving or valuing yourself enough to even allow yourself to know what you love to do.) So how do you find out what you love to do? The exercise below will assist you in getting clear on what you love to do. You may repeat this process as many times as you wish to gain refinement, so approach it confidently, knowing you have as many chances as you want.

Exercise to Find What You Love to Do

1. Make a list of 3 to 5 things you absolutely love to do. Choose only things that excite you just to think of doing them! Do not judge these things. Just write them down.

2. Now pick one item from the list. (You can repeat later so you do not have to make a final choice right now.) Choose what feels like the most important or favorite item

3. Make a list of the ways you might express the item in #2. List as many ways as you can think of. Do this again every day or so, allowing new ideas to flow in without judging the ideas. Keep this list in a separate notebook. You will be surprised at the creative ideas that come to you as you continue to do this. Creative Mind is unlimited and, as part of the Universe,you are unlimited.

17

Your Purpose in Life

*"If an experience has purpose, it has meaning.
If it has no purpose, it has no meaning — it is
then just a scattering of energies around an
experience."*　　　　　　　　　Arnold Patent

Knowing that you can create whatever you truly
want in your life through Alpha-level Concentration
and the other processes in this book, it now becomes
very important to have clarity about your purpose in
life. Not being clear about your purpose is like travelling
in a foreign country without a map — even if you arrived
at your destination, you probably would not know it.
And having a clearly stated purpose for your life will
give meaning that is otherwise lacking.

When you complete the process in this chapter, you
will have stated in words a joyful expression of your
purpose in life. Unlike a goal, your purpose is not
something you will reach and surpass. It is, rather, the
broad framework or context for all of your life — your
purpose for living. It is important to make it very grand,
very magnificent, for it is true that each of us is here for
a very grand purpose: to remember our true identity as
creative beings. We are not these bodies, personalities,
minds and emotions we identify with; we are the light,
the energy behind these forms.

All my life I have played a little game with my mind:
I transform people and things in my mind to be more

than they appear to be! For instance, if I would see a poor, stooped, unshaven old man standing on the corner in tattered, dirty clothes, I would transform him in my mind to an upright, resourceful, healthy, wealthy man of confidence and ability. In the flash of an instant, I would imagine that he was dressed in the most elegant, tasteful suit, groomed and polished from head to toe! His face then radiated relaxation and well-being as though he enjoyed each moment of his day!

This game was not something I thought about or took time to make up beforehand; rather it just "happened" as I would glance at a person or thing (like a building or a littered vacant lot). I never told anyone about this game when I was small; I did not realize then that it meant anything. But later in life as I grew to understand how creative thought is, I realized that I was actually affecting the energy around that person or thing by my thoughts and imaginings!

I have included this story in this particular chapter because I believe that with your thoughts, you are having either a negative or a positive effect not only on your life, but also on the world around you. Begin watching your thoughts and the judgments you make and realize that you are either helping or hurting by the nature and quality of your thoughts! By making a commitment now to define your purpose, you will become more and more consciously aware of your thoughts and more responsible with the energy you are directing toward others. This will directly contribute to the betterment of the whole planet.

So begin to define your very grand purpose. Pretending that you have no limitations of any kind, allow yourself to begin sensing what that purpose is. Allow yourself to go through the process of defining and redefining it. When you have honed it and refined it and it fits you well, it will act like a magnet to pull you toward it, giving meaning to all you do.

Discovering Your Purpose

1. List 5 to 10 personality traits that you like most about yourself (For example: my integrity, my compassion, my sense of humor).
2. Now list 5 to 10 ways you really enjoy expressing yourself (e.g., singing, cooking, writing, speaking).
3. Briefly write a description of your idea of a perfect world, stated in positive terms. (e.g., lavish abundance, perfect health and unconditional love for and with everyone).
4. Now write a sentence using 2 or (at most) 3 items from each of #1, #2 and #3. (As an example: "To use my (1) *intuition and clear self-expression* in (2) *speaking and writing* to enjoy (3) *unconditional love, robust health and lavish abundance* with everyone.")

You may want to revise your stated purpose several times over a period of time until you are completely satisfied with it. The shorter it is, the more powerful it will be in your life. When you finally arrive at a statement that really expresses your true purpose, you will know it clearly and will feel very expanded by it.

Once arrived at, you may want to write it on 3x5 cards and place it around your home or in your automobile so you will read it often. Repeat it to yourself and experience that it draws you toward its manifestation.

When you have a purpose that is truly right for you, it will help you make decisions and stay more directed in your life — more "on purpose." I sometimes experience when making a decision that it becomes easier as soon as I ask myself, "Is this in alignment with my purpose?" If that answer is no, I decline whatever "opportunity" may be presented to me since I am committed to aligning everything in my life with my purpose.

It is very important that the thought of your purpose bring you so much joy that you will gladly dedicate your life to its fulfillment. The greater the intensity of your passionate dedication to your purpose, the more surely your intentions will be brought into manifestation.

Exercise to Fulfill Your Life's Purpose

Sit comfortably erect with spine straight. Close your eyes and turn your inward gaze toward the mid-spot between the eyebrows. Breathe deeply and relax, allowing yourself to enter a more peaceful level.

Imagine that you are expressing yourself according to each aspect of your stated life's purpose. Visualize it all in specific detail. Be aware of how you are dressed, how it feels to rest comfortably in your body, noticing the smells and sights all around you. Feel an expansion of love in your heart area, as you express according to your purpose.

Experience pleasure as you realize that your gifts and talents are unique and are a blessing to yourself and to others. You are essential to this world; no one can fill the role you are here to play as well as you. Now mentally repeat to yourself, "This is my purpose in living."

Feel the joy that floods your consciousness in knowing and fulfilling your purpose. Continue to feel this joy as you prepare to return to normal waking consciousness. Allow yourself to continue feeling this joy for as long as possible.

Affirmations:

1. *The perfect plan for my life is now manifesting.*

2. *I am healthy, wealthy and happy fulfilling my Life Purpose.*

3. *The more my activities align with my Life Purpose, the happier, healthier and richer I am.*

4. *I work for God; money works for me!*

5. *I am centered and on purpose in all my activities.*

18

Integrity

*"To thine own self be true, and it shall
follow as the night the day, thou canst
not then be false to any man."*
William Shakespeare

Energy is the essence of everything in Universe,
including the material world. We have seen in other
sections of this book how even a solid, inanimate object
like a wooden table appears less and less solid as its
surface is viewed through increasing microscopic intensity. The molecules of its energy are so arranged
that its physical appearance, however, is that of solid-
ity. Similarly we know that matter which is released
through nuclear fission instantaneously reverts back
to energy.

What this tells us is that the essence of everything,
whether a wooden table or a human being, is energy.
Understanding gained about one thing can be instruc-
tive about another because of the common essential
energy basis. But what does this have to do with the
subject of Integrity? Let us look further.

One of the most important issues on Planet Earth
today is that of how to handle nuclear fission. It has
become very apparent that, regardless of whether it is
used as weaponry or as a source of energy, we cannot
deal with nuclear power using old rules. New rules
must apply, new understanding must be gained, if our
planetary family is to survive and flourish.

And if you are to live your life powerfully, you must understand the Universal laws that govern life in this age. The guidelines by which many of our parents and grandparents lived are becoming less and less workable. This is not to dishonor our ancestors but to understand that many of them functioned the best they could and frequently in a lot of ignorance. We have more understanding available today, more "light" and just as in the field of communications, we must update our abilities if we are to function successfully.

New Capability Requires New Ground Rules

If you switch from driving a horse and wagon to a Maserati, a corresponding shift in awareness must occur. Even half asleep, you could probably go along safely in a wagon. But at higher speeds, successful operation depends on a wide-awake, skillful driver and a precision vehicle. In consciousness today, we are moving from the wagon to the Maserati; our awareness and our skills must augment accordingly. What could slip by without wreaking havoc yesterday will not hold up under the stress of today's faster speeds. Like it or not, we are dealing with energy in a more direct and powerful way now.

Recognizing that everything is energy helps us to realize that integrity is indispensable. If you are dealing with energy, what else could possibly work? If you strip a thing to its bare essentials, what pretense can survive? Lack of integrity can only exist in illusion. If you are dealing with essence itself, illusion is impossible.

In recent years increasing numbers of Western men and women have begun to meditate as a way to expand consciousness and live fuller, more meaningful lives. Anyone experiencing this expanded awareness knows with certainty that everything is energy and that, if integrity is lacking, the whole foundation will be faulty.

Integrity is indispensable if you are to operate the vehicle of your life as required in the faster vibration of our times. The increased power resulting from alignment in consciousness which you will gain from living in integrity may well surprise you. Energy will be freed up for creative expression in your life, energy that may now be required to hold down suppressions of negative energy. Whether those suppressions are the anger of unexpressed, hidden resentments, for instance, or those resulting from living in a less-than-authentic way stemming from unacceptance of yourself, you will feel a great surge of life force energy when you clear the channel of your life of any lack of integrity.

Increasing Your Integrity

Shown here are just a few of the ways you could be out of integrity, perhaps without even realizing that an integrity issue is involved. Cleaning up these areas may feel a little frightening because you will be disturbing the status quo, but you will reap wonderful benefits in greater aliveness and joy as soon as you undertake the process.

1. Staying in a relationship which is dead and in which you and your partner have ceased to learn and grow because of fear or guilt.

2. Flattering someone because it is the socially acceptable thing to do.

3. Being unwilling to express an angry feeling and living in resentment toward a person or situation when you could "clear the air" by sending safe, direct "I-messages."

4. Working at a job you do not like solely for the sake of earning money and resenting the job and your employer because of your predicament.

5. Blaming anyone or anything for any situation in your life. The only truthful way is to own responsibility yourself (without blaming yourself either!) for creating your life the way it is. Remember, if you don't like it, you can change it by applying the techniques in this book.

6. Playing the role of victim, persecutor, rescuer or rescuee. It doesn't matter one bit which side of the axis you take; if you're in the game, you are keeping it going! Choose out! You can choose happiness instead!

7. Accepting consciously that you are limited IN ANY WAY! If you insist on having limitations in your life, at least start saying,"I am a powerful being and I choose these limitations." (This makes it easy for you to choose otherwise when you get ready to have it be different.)

8. Accepting consciously that someone else is limited in any way (feeling sorry for him). This is disempowering to yourself and the other person. Instead, you can remind yourself quietly that "everyone is as powerful as everyone else" and know that that person is just using his free will to choose what he wants right now. When he is ready to choose something else, he will!

9. Wanting to convert or preach to others because you want them to believe or understand as you do. Remember that everyone is already perfect and has a right to choose where he wants to be. If you really want to help, silently know the truth for that person, smile and keep it a secret!

10. Treating another person in any way you would not want to be treated! The Golden Rule is so simple and subtly reminds you that the other person is you!

Affirmations:

1. *I am loved and supported in total integrity.*
2. *The greater my level of integrity, the happier my life becomes.*
3. *My connection to the love and power of the Infinite flows through the channel of total integrity.*
4. *Integrity is the essence of my success.*
5. *My life works beautifully because it is filled with integrity.*

19

Life is a School

"The only failure is not to participate."
Marshall Thurber

One of the most liberating attitudes you can have is the understanding that you are on this planet to learn. This will enable you to experience success in literally everything you undertake because you will either achieve what you wanted to or you will learn something. In either case the experience will contribute to your progress. This distinction alone removes the great suffering that people inflict upon themselves when they believe that each learning experience is a big mistake.

Life is really a vast school. At almost every turn, there are lessons to be learned and we learn by trial and error. We easily accept this for the very young. When a baby begins learning to walk, he will fall repeatedly before he masters the skill. Adults are supportive and encouraging of the baby while he is "practicing," aware that he will fall and get up and fall again and again — knowing that he will *try until* he can walk well. And, for the child, we continue applying the successful model of "trying until" a skill is learned for talking, climbing, riding a bike, drawing letters and numerals and a thousand other skills. Consequently, most all children learn all these tasks very adequately.

At some point of growth, however, we seem to decide unconsciously that it is no longer okay to make a mistake, that we must "get it right the first time." Practicing, therefore, must cease. And the way to excellence in just about any endeavor is practice or experimentation! Under these parameters you cannot play for the joy of playing — now you must win! It is no longer acceptable just to participate fully; you must perform exceptionally well or be considered a failure. It is like requiring yourself to hit the bull's eye without the opportunity to practice with a bow and arrow. Albert Einstein observed that so frequently a childlike abandon accompanies great discoveries and inventions in science and other fields. With the necessity of playing to win, however, this natural childlike quality is lost.

Imagine the brain power available to NASA. And yet the first moon shot was off course 97% of the time! The space vehicle was apparently headed toward its mark only 3% of the time, but it was on course when it landed! The lunar voyage was composed primarily of correcting the course.

And yet we still seem to believe that we should perform with little or no error and that if we have more information, more knowledge or more intelligence, we will be able to turn in a perfect performance. Nothing could be further from the truth and if we could make life work that way, it would defeat the very purpose of life anyway!

For the purpose of life is to learn, but somewhere along the line we human beings have adopted the idea that we are here to turn in a good performance. We have forgotten that we are practicing and that mistakes are not failures but only indicate the area where we need improvement.

"We are deliberately designed to learn only by trial and error. We're brought up to think that nobody should make mistakes. Most children get de-geniused by the love and fear of their parents . . . that they might make a mistake. But all my advances were made by mistakes. You uncover what is when you discover what isn't."

Buckminster Fuller

Forgiveness, the Master Eraser

Forgiveness plays such an important role in succeeding in this school of life, especially the willingness to forgive yourself when you have made a mistake. Being too hard on yourself for making a mistake is the biggest obstacle to correcting it. If a 5th grader earns a perfect score throughout the year, it means he was in the wrong grade! More than likely he belonged in the 6th grade!

If you are "turning in a perfect performance" in your life, the chances are you are not stretching yourself and moving toward and beyond the boundaries of your comfort zone. Most likely you are "playing it safe," avoiding risks as much as possible. Whether or not you are consciously aware of it, you probably have the idea that the purpose of life is to be comfortable and avoid confronting anything that frightens or threatens you.

Are You Living or Surviving?

If your focus in life is to play in the safe zone and avoid risk and fear, then you are surviving. If you are surviving, you are not living. And if you are living, you are not surviving. And surviving is less meaningful than we usually think anyway. You might want to ask yourself the following question: "Am I here to extend my

193

life as long as possible even if that means sacrificing the quality of my life experience? Or is it my purpose to live a life filled with the greatest quality I am capable of regardless of its length?" I suggest you stop right now and give yourself time to really think in depth about these two questions. Think about a person or persons, living or dead, whom you most admire. What do you most admire about them? Is it that you admire the quality of their life regardless of how old they were at death? Are any of them people whose life was lived avoiding risks? Has it ever occurred to you that quality rather than quantity applies to life itself? What changes will it make in your experience if you truly accept that it is the quality of your life that counts?

Please be aware that I am not recommending that you become a daredevil in any way; I am certainly not a daredevil and yet I consistently push out the boundaries of my limitations in as many ways as I can. Even though I teach people how to walk barefoot across burning hot coals in The Firewalk, I am not a daredevil! That workshop, instead, is all about showing others how they can reach for more of what they want to achieve in their lives and do it without harm to themselves or anyone else. And they will have to confront the boundaries of their limitations and face some of their fears to accomplish that!

In the next chapter, we will deal in detail with specific techniques for facing fear and removing limitations.

20

Facing Fear

"Fearlessness is the first requisite of spirituality.
Cowards can never be moral."
                                    Mahatma Gandhi

Facing fear instead of avoiding it is a powerful experience. For what you will discover is that your fears are just thoughts and feelings which you have been embuing with great emotional charge. Robbed of the energy you have been investing in them, those fears are meaningless. You will experience that as long as you run from fear, it will seem very threatening; but when you head toward it, the terrifying fear dragon turns into a paper tiger and becomes lifeless, like a punctured balloon sputtering to the ground. Fear does nothing to help you avoid the thing you fear, anyway; all it does is weaken your will. When you head toward your fear, determined to prevail, it will evaporate right before your eyes!

My life was dramatically changed the first time I experienced The Firewalk. I knew several people who had attended previous firewalk workshops and my attitude was: "if they can do it, I can do it!" I really did not think that I would be very afraid. However, as the hour approached for the workshop to begin, I noticed a nervousness in my body and awareness that I had not anticipated. Then when the big bonfire was lit, it was so hot that we could not stand anywhere near it! I wasn't scared; I was terrified! I would never have believed that I would feel so much fear!

This took place in Colorado, in a beautiful meadow surrounded by three mountains. The indoor part of the workshop was being conducted in a huge tent with over 200 people present. After about two hours, I needed to go to the bathroom. During a short break, I headed through tall weeds up a steep hill toward some portable restrooms. (As inconvenient as it was to reach the toilets, I was determined not to add the handicap of a full bladder to my fear of the fire!) It was very dark and suddenly, struggling through the waist-high weeds, the ground fell out from under me and I plunged straight down for about eight feet! "Oh my God! Rattlesnakes!" My greatest fear all my life has been of snakes and my mind went wild in the first few seconds with the thought that I had plunged into a shallow shaft of some kind. And this was in July in the Rockies — a perfect time and place for rattlesnakes! Frantically, I felt along the wall of the shaft with my hands. Rough vertical wooden timbers as high as I could reach! Indeed this was not a natural crevice or ditch but a constructed shaft of some kind!

I usually perform fairly well under stress and then fall apart after the crisis has passed — and this time was no exception. I immediately began yelling for help and in just a minute or so, two men (whom I regarded as no less than rescuing angels!) pulled me out of that pit.* And I still had not gone to the restroom!

---

*Upon later reflection it occurred to me that the Universe had afforded me an opportunity to face my fear of snakes at this time, too, for I experienced all this as though there were snakes in that shaft. If, however, there were any snakes in there with me, they did not touch me.

That accomplished, I headed back into the big tent where the workshop was already again in progress. I was bloody, dirty and thoroughly shaken up and no one had even missed me! I struggled to take in every word the leader spoke, wondering what I had missed and whether it was a "critical piece," the absence of which would cause me somehow to burn my feet. There was no opportunity to ask such questions. Soon we were led out to the fire which was raked into a 10-foot long bed of glowing coals! I wanted to get it over with and jumped right into line . . . and then just could not bring myself to step into that fire.

For the next hour I went through more terror than I have ever before experienced! There was every form of fear I could imagine and then some. My mind raced to my little daughter, barely 9 years old. My thoughts besieged me, "This is irresponsible, Christina. Even if you are crazy enough to do this, you don't have the right to injure yourself so that you cannot care for Julie!" And on and on my fears assaulted me! Finally, I decided not to do the firewalk. "I don't have to do this," I thought. "It's okay not to do it. I don't have to prove anything. I can't afford to do this to Julie!"

Now it is true that I have never consciously run from a fear in my life. And as I dealt with choosing not to face those fears, I felt overwhelmingly heavy and burdened. I realized right then that I had been carrying around all this fear, now conscious, and that if I did not face it, I would have to carry it consciously for the rest of my life. At that point, I knew that I would prefer to die rather than not face these fears! As I reflected on this new awareness, I gazed out into the darkness of the meadow and spontaneously imagined my dead body being covered up with a white sheet. I felt calm and peaceful. Yes, I truly would rather die than run from my fears!

My breathing became deeper and freer - and more powerful. Interiorizing my consciousness further, I asked my Higher Self, "Is it okay for me to do this?" Instantly I received a strong, clear "YES!" My energy became even more centered and I felt a warm sensation begin to spread throughout my body, experiencing awe and gratitude for the miracle I was living. I asked just one more question: "Will you do this for me?" The answer was as rapid and distinct as before: "YES!" A burst of powerful energy shot through my whole body and psyche as I lifted my eyes toward the sky and stepped into the burning coal bed. A few short steps and I was on the other side, never to be quite the same again!

In the week that followed I experienced repeatedly that I felt lighter and more limitless in my thoughts, feelings and actions. It was like suddenly being a new person on the inside, making all the difference on the outside. A week later, I had another opportunity to walk across the burning coals — this time it was 25 feet across — and those old fears did not arise. This all happened several years ago and it is my experience that I have been changed and permanently benefitted by this one experience of facing fears. Because of this model of facing my fears, I have reached many goals in my life that I may not otherwise even have attempted, including the writing and publication of this book!

The Firewalk is a powerful opportunity to transform your fears into dreams come true. If you are experiencing any lack in any area of your life, the chances are that you have suppressed fear, which can be dealt with quickly and effectively by participating in this powerful experience!

An anagram for the word "fear" which helps to put it into better perspective and discharge some of the emotional energy which we invest in it is:

F alse
E vidence
A ppearing
R eal

When you go toward a fear and experience that it dissolves or breaks down under the power of your courage and intention, you will have a different grasp of what I mean when I say that "fear is not real." Unless and until you have this experience, this will probably sound like an "aerie faerie" statement. But it is literally true that, like other emotions that only appear to be real, fear will not stand up under a strong opposing belief. It appears real only so long as it remains unchallenged by the power of your mind!

The exercise below is a 5-step process for dealing effectively with fear. If you apply the steps to the story of my first firewalk, you will see that I went through each of these steps (although I was unaware at the moment of what I was doing).

Exercise

1. Identify the fear. Breathe and feel it. Tell yourself the truth about it!

2. Analyze it to death! What does the fear feel like? What, specifically, are you afraid of? Can you learn more about the object of your fear? Remember that we usually fear the unknown in one form or another; by becoming familiar with the thing you are afraid of, you will remove most of the emotional charge around it, allowing you to become more rational and less

compulsive. Find out everything you possibly can about the object of your fear.

3. Be willing to accept the worst. If you keep examining your fear, you will quickly discover what to you is "the worst." When you can find some way to accept that, you can move on to the next step. (Note: I was able to do this at my first firewalk by default, i.e., I decided that I "would rather die" than run from my fear.)

4. Be willing to accept and expect the best. Take your time with this one; it may not be as easy as you would think at first glance. Are you truly willing to expect to have in your life the wonderful things you say you want? What if you feel unworthy to have so much happiness, so much prosperity, so much love? You might find that you sabotage yourself in some way. This step requires clearing yourself of negative thoughts and beliefs just as much as dealing directly with fear issues. Use Alpha Concentration, Connected Breathing, Meditation and Affirmation to clear and heal yourself.

5. Take action! As soon as you get through the first four steps CONGRUENTLY, it is important to take action immediately. Reinforce your positive efforts by moving confidently toward your chosen goal. It is helpful to remember a story from the Old Testament wherein the "walls of Jericho" fell only as the invading army reached them, sounding the triumphant trumpet blast — and not a second before! The thing you fear may APPEAR to stand steadfast until the last moment but if your intention is firm and focused, it will collapse before you.

21

Living with Enthusiasm

*One of the aspects of genius is
the ability to light one's own fire.*

When you live enthusiastically, allowing all of your feelings to flow through you and into your activities, you draw on a great reservoir of Universal life force energy to enliven every moment of your life. Time spent feeling guilty over the past and fearful about the future is wasted. You can do nothing about either the past or the future.

The only moment you have is now. If you withhold part of your energy or part of your attention so that you are performing an activity absentmindedly, you are robbing that moment and that activity of your life force. It is unloving to yourself and to other people to withhold yourself.

If you discover that part of your attention is drawn elsewhere, it is important for you to clear your consciousness. Otherwise you will be distracted, preoccupied — generally "absent." You may achieve this clearing by talking with a friend who knows how to listen well or with a counselor who is loving and accepting, or you may be fortunate enough to find a Rebirther to help you clear the static from your consciousness very quickly.

I cannot overemphasize the importance of clearing away the blockages that prevent you from being as powerful as you can be. Holding in any problem is like attempting to hold an inflated rubber boat under water; you have to keep at it every moment and the second you let go, up it pops. Living with suppressions is a tremendous drain on your energy and will keep you from achieving your goals, from relating happily with others and will rob you of your peace of mind.

The process below will help you get into the present moment when you find yourself withdrawn or absent.

Exercise

1. Breathe and relax.
2. Allow yourself to become aware of what you are feeling. Be honest with yourself. What is REALLY going on?
3. If you are judging or condemning yourself or anyone else in any way, forgive that now. Forgive yourself. Forgive the other person(s).
4. Experience love for yourself and others. Feel it throughout your body. Don't move on to the next step until you actually feel love for that person.* Commit to holding onto that feeling of love as much as possible as you go about your day.
5. Look about you and notice what and who is present in this moment. Be willing to express your love toward that person or thing in any way that feels appropriate.
6. Keep breathing and enjoy your connection to the loving energy of the Universe.

*You may find it more difficult to forgive yourself than to forgive another person. Until you do forgive and love yourself, however, you will continue to create negative experiences in your life.

22

Trusting Your Body

*"You are an incredible, God-like being whose
only limitation is the way in which you perceive
yourself and the reality in which you live."*
Peggy Dylan Burkan

There is a critical moment in the Firewalk workshop when everyone listens with both ears. It is the moment when we discuss how each person can know if it is appropriate to walk across those burning coals. It is not unusual for people to have difficulty with ordinary decisions, but when fear is present and there is a potential confrontation with something as big and frightening as burning hot coals, one may easily feel paralyzed. The chattering voices in the mind all compete for attention and the fear level rises higher and higher. One voice says, "Don't do it; you'll get hurt." Another says, "If others can do it, so can I!" Yet another voice says, "What am I doing here anyway? Maybe these people are all crazy." Still another says, "If I don't do this, I'll feel like a failure again!" By this time you may feel fairly rattled. How do you know which voice to listen to? Which one should you trust?

You don't listen to any of them; you listen to your body! Your body will tell you if it is appropriate or not for you to walk into that burning coal bed. And, if you can trust your body to guide you in something as outrageous as walking across burning hot coals, don't you imagine that you could trust it to give you accurate feedback on other decisions, too? What if you could rely on your body energy to guide you in your next business decision? Or how about tuning into what is really going on with a person in your life — perhaps your child? Imagine the difference in a political election when enough of us voters can tune into the energy of the candidates to know clearly which one has integrity, who intends to render high service or which contender is seeking only personal aggrandizement. Just as Kirlian photography can take photos of a human aura and show areas of disease before it reaches the level of the physical body, you can tune into your own body energy for timely information in all areas of your life.

In order to tune into the body, we must become much more still than we have been in our hectic, overscheduled lives. In his excellent book, <u>Money is My Friend</u>, my friend, Phil Laut suggests staying in bed for one entire day every week, tuning into your deeper self and writing affirmations. I took the advice to heart and practiced this faithfully for a period of months when I first began experiencing the rebirthing process. It brought up my fears of being considered lazy, being unproductive, not being able to afford to stay in bed and other concerns. But, having experienced it, I join with Phil in recommending this valuable practice. Becoming more sensitive to your body knowledge requires a willingness to listen and learn, to be flexible and responsive to the information thus received. It necessitates an awareness that you are not a separate being, but that you are connected to all the energy of the Universe and, thus, connected to all other forms of life, animate and inanimate. It requires letting go of any position of "I want to be right" and flowing with an attitude of "which direction do I take next?" You may need to ask yourself, "Would I rather be right than happy?" "Am I just interested in getting the credit for something or am I concerned with the overall results?" When you let go of thinking of yourself as a separate creature, then you can begin to tune into your body and the incredible guidance system already operating in the natural Universe.

It is an amazing phenomenon that, if you are "on track," your body will become quiet and peaceful even though the hurdle you are facing may be ostensibly frightening. And your body will signal you strongly when something is amiss, even though that something may appear entirely harmless to your conscious mind. This factor impressed me strongly the first time I led The Firewalk. I thought that if ever I would feel a little nervous and preoccupied, it would be the few days preceding that event. After all, leading a whole group of people across burning hot coals is quite an undertaking. However, my actual experience was that I was as calm as a cucumber and felt entirely "present" at all times. I felt light and happy and had a lot of fun preparing for that workshop. And, of course, everything went smoothly.

On the other hand I have experienced having my body send me all kinds of negative signals when I was just going to meet someone at a coffee shop. My solar plexus will contract or I may feel a heaviness around my heart or, more often, something in my chest will seem stuck. These are my signals. Yours will be all your own. It doesn't matter what they are; it just matters that you be able to listen and tune in to what your body energy is telling you.

Your physical body energy will correlate and interface with your emotional body and with your mind and intuition. They are all related and interconnected. You may get a body feeling, then a flash of an image followed by a sound or words and maybe also a sense of knowingness about something. Learning to trust these messages enough to slip into lower gear will bring more information. No matter how fast you are moving in the physical world, you can calm yourself inside by slowing and connecting your breathing for a few moments. Anytime you are in unknown terrain, it helps to take it a little slower until you are clear about the next direction to take. With patience, your hunch will be verified one way or the other and you will learn to trust the next messages more naturally and easily.

Learning to tap into the interconnected information available through the body, emotions, mind and intuition assists in all areas of life, including commerce, long approached by Westerners as purely left-brained and logical. Look, however, at what is happening in the international economy today. Japan leads the world in so many areas of accomplishment; this is not surprising, for the Japanese people have long valued the use of both sides of the brain. They apply themselves diligently in the workaday world and also allow regular time for meditation and other right-brain functions. They honor parts of themselves beyond the little conscious mind, not only as individuals, but as corporations. Realizing that a company is only as good as its workers, Japanese businesses set aside time and rooms for meditation and still other rooms for venting anger, frustration and other negative feelings experienced by workers. The Western cultures would be wise to model this attitude of doing as much as possible as individuals and tuning into the wholeness of expanded mind for more energy, thus covering all the bases. Some of the more forward-looking U.S. corporations are beginning to include these elements now.

I often think of human beings as pieces of battery-operated equipment; it is vitally necessary to reconnect to the power source to recharge if the energy is to remain strong in the individual. Attempting to function without connection to the higher energy source leads to the disease and addiction rampant in our society today, wherein countless numbers feel so separate and alone.

Your Body Never Lies!

When the idea of listening to your body is first suggested, it may sound preposterous. But please read on. We have this marvelous instrument, the physical body, which is capable of so very much more than we have realized. Just as the mind and brain is capable of far more than we have realized, so is the body. The body has the capability of functioning in a superphysical way as an extension of the mind and the intuition beyond the five physical senses.

From the moment of human conception, the formation of a human body goes through stages recalling first the one-celled amoeba, then through the tadpole stage, then the fish stage and on up through the higher mammalian stages until finally, completely formed at full term, a human infant emerges. Inherent in the brain's development through all those stages are intrinsic capabilities for primitive instinct and primordial sensing that are way outside the ranges of our five physical senses. We all have ancient knowing. Maybe we can learn to sense colors with our fingertips, to feel rain before clouds appear, and maybe even to call the rain down when needed. With training, we begin at a body level to "remember" how to exercise these capabilities and many others beyond our present recall.

We know, for instance, that in the hours before an earthquake or other natural disturbance, wildlife and domestic animals alike sense something amiss in the environment and behave erratically. Perhaps this also applies to radiation. Perhaps it also applies to pollutants so that in the future we will not have to wait to discover the harmful presence of a poison only after our population has been exposed to it.

Our evolution has brought us, as a planetary family, to our present level. We are coming out of dark times into much more light. The old ways of sticking to the status quo and waiting for any small change to happen gradually over comfortable eons of time (so we don't have to stir out of our drowsiness to adapt to it!) are over. If we are to keep up with what is going on at every level of activity on Planet Earth, we must begin accessing and using more of ourselves at higher levels. It is high time to begin listening to the body. The vibration of Mother Earth is speeding up and we must quicken our vibration correspondingly or perish. It is our task to begin ridding ourselves of outmoded habits and belief systems that no longer work and begin the process of rediscovering our true identity as Light!

In the Western, industrialized and now high-tech world we have relied so much on the little separate, conscious mind to "figure everything out." And the conscious mind was never equal to that task. It doesn't have the capacity to operate that way. It is designed to be an instrument only, an instrument to receive information from the higher mind. But we have forgotten all this and we attempt to operate with the little conscious mind running everything. The results speak for themselves. We make an advance in one area — smallpox is wiped off the face of the Earth, a vaccine is found for polio — and a bigger collective bogeyman rears its ugly head. The nuclear threat has hung over our heads for more than a generation already. And the dreaded AIDS is yet another loud signal that we must alter the ways we go about our lives. We are constantly reminded that no one is immune; we can no longer separate off "the group that is to blame" and point an accusing finger as a way to remain in a delusion of isolated safety for "me and mine."

The second stanza to the age-old dictatorial cry, "Divide and conquer!" is a cacophonous echo, "Separate and die!" Indeed if we are to survive, we must begin to realize that we are not separate, that we are part of the same energy, the same light that is the essence of each human being and all other life. It is time for us to begin listening to all the signals we possibly can as individuals. Can we ignore the messages any longer and expect to survive? As individuals, we must begin to honor all the dimensions of ourselves if we are to be healthy and balanced. When enough individuals have reached this level, we will tip the scale for our planetary family as a whole. Will you add your weight to the critical mass now accumulating?

Here are some steps you can take to begin training yourself to tune into the expansion that will result from learning to trust your magnificent body instrument.

1. **MEDITATION.** Begin a meditation routine. Even a few minutes morning and evening will bring major benefits into your life. Read the chapter on Meditation in this book and use that or another meditation which works for you. The important element is regular, consistent practice. And don't judge the results; just begin following a meditation routine and observe your life experience.

2. **AFFIRMATION.** Begin changing your thought patterns and the ways in which you carry on your inner and outer dialogue by use of Affirmation. You are creating your life with each choice you make, with each statement you make whether to yourself or someone else. You can have anything you like if you are willing to make the required changes in thought and energy patterns.

3. **CONNECTED BREATHING/REBIRTHING.** Begin clearing your energy field of suppressed negative emotions through Connected Breathing. Remember that it is fine to talk about what is wrong, to discuss "where the muddy spots may be," as is done in traditional psychotherapy. But sooner or later you must "get into the bath" to actually do the cleanup. You cannot clear your energy field without getting into the energy! You cannot stay tightly in control with your little conscious mind and succeed in getting this work done. You cannot acccomplish this clearing by simply understanding it mentally; you must go beyond your head, beyond your cognitive processes, and expand into your heart space. Certainly you will feel vulnerable but it is a thrilling, alive process and you can be assured you will be safe no matter how unsafe it may feel at times. A caring, skilled rebirther or other conscious professional who is trained to work at the energy level, can provide priceless support and assistance, helping you to quickly move through resistance.

4. **FACING YOUR FEARS.** If you find yourself in fear, you can move out of it and back into love. Learn an effective model for facing your fears and moving through them to the other side. The Firewalk is the best way I know, which is why I lead it. But any way you achieve it is fine, as long as you can use the model repeatedly to get through your fears as they arise.

Last Words

The Humble-Bee
"Wiser far than human seer,
Yellow-breeched philospher!
Seeing only what is fair,
Sipping only what is sweet,
Thou dost mock at fate and care,
Leave the chaff, and take the wheat."
Ralph Waldo Emerson

If I were to leave you with one thought only, it would be that of realizing that the single most important element in any of our lives is where we place our attention from moment to moment.

As a divine energy being residing in the vehicle of the physical body with a mind to use as an instrument, you are ever creating out of the raw material of thought essence.

Choose consciously what you will create by paying attention only to that which you would have more of in your life.

Coal stroll confronts fears feet-first

Firewalks light way to self-improvement

By William Thomas
Staff Reporter

Terrified, Karen King stands at the edge of the fire, unable to move.

A 32-year-old Memphis mother, she has paid $100 to walk on blistering-hot coals in the belief it will somehow improve her. But now that the time has come, she cannot take the first step for fear of losing her sole - both of them.

The fire stretches out in front of her for eight or nine feet. It has been kindled in a remote farmyard, east of Eads, Tenn., next to a large barn. It is nearly midnight, and Mrs. King, who is barefoot and wearing rolled-up jeans and a sweatshirt, shivers int he December air.

She is surrounded by people who hold hands and sing about a river that is flowing and growing. At the far end of the bed of coals stands a blue-eyed blond woman in a pink jumpsuit. Around her neck is a large crystal. Somewhere in her 30s, she occasionally holds out her arms and silently exhorts the frightened Mrs. King to hotfoot it across the fire.

The woman in pink is Christina Thomas of Memphis, a leader of self-improvement workshops. Friday night, she conducted the "firewalk" - likely the first ever held in West Tennessee. It attracted a mixed bag of people that included two lawyers, a teacher, a minister, a computer programmer, a skin-care consultant and a marketing representative.

Although ritual firewalks have been held in various parts of the world throughout history, they became popular in California in 1984 as exercises in self-improvement. Would-be firewalkers have paid as much as $350 for a chance to cross a bed of coals barefoot and prove to themselves that fear is nothing but a self-limiting illusion.

Mrs. Thomas, who has walked on fire more than 120 times, follows in the footsteps of most Western firewalkers who use the ancient practice as a way of subordinating fear to will. And that, she insists, can change your life.

"Once in a very great while," Mrs. Thomas told her follows, "life gives you one centimeter of opportunity. If you are able to step into that, your life will never be the same again. This workshop can be that for you. Truly, your life will never be the same."

Although none of the participants believed at the outset that they could walk across coals without burning their feet, most of them said they believed they could learn something about themselves by facing what Mrs. Thomas calls "the combat zone."

"I'm afraid I'll walk and afraid I won't," said Lawyer John Colton. "I like to be involved in things like this because I want to know more about myself. I don't think I'm afraid of the fire as much as I'm afraid of failure."

Jeana Lightfoot, marketing representative, admitted that "it didn't sound like a lot of fun when I first heard about it. But I think the only thing that limits me is me - and I'd like to change that if I can."

Joy Young, skin-care consultant, said, "I know it's crazy, but I want to be all I can be. I was scared to come here. But I'm excited, too, and I want to see what happens."

Lawyer Tim Schaeffer, who allowed the firewalkers to use his farm, said he was there as an observer because he knew that it was impossible for flesh to be exposed to coals of 1,200 degrees F without burning. "I just don't believe it can be done," he said, "I want to see 'em try." Before the night was over, Schaeffer took off his shoes and also crossed the fire.

a

Burning faith

Photographs by Lisa Waddell

Right: John Colton looks to the sky, repeating "cool moss, cool moss," drawing courage for his "firewalk" across the hot coals.

It was more a test of confidence than endurance - stepping barefoot across hot coals on an Eads, Tenn., farm Friday night. The goal of Leader Christina Thomas was self-improvement, pushing the participants beyond their fears and personal limits through a test of faith that the smoldering embers would not burn their feet. All came through unscathed and unscorched in an experience Ms. Thomas said would change their lives. Story on Page A1.

Mrs. Thomas gave daughter Julie a hug after the youngster made the firewalk, her second.

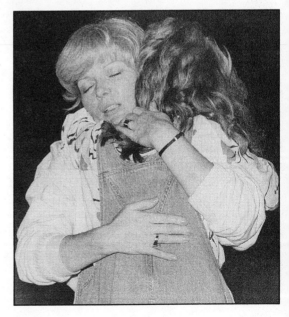

b

Photographs by Lisa Waddell

Above:
At the beginning of the "firewalk", Christina Thomas lit the fire that burned for several hours and the participants gathered around hoilding hands as thecoals were scattered to create the glowing path.

Right:
Christina Thomas leads the way across the fiery path.

c

Since firewalks became popular in the United States, scientists have put forth a number of theories explaining how humans can walk across a bed of coals without getting burned.

Professional firewalkers - and that includes Christina Thomas - insist that they don't know why some people can walk on coals without getting burned. Mrs. Thomas points out that it has nothing to do with the purpose of the firewalk, anyway.

"This is not about firewalking," she says, "this is about fear. We're having a real fire tonight. The reality of the coals is right there in front of you. This is a way to set up a big obstacle so that these people can experience real fear. Now, if they can just go through that fear, they will be changed. They will discover that they are more than they think they are."

To set up the fear, Mrs. Thomas leads the group into the yard to light the wood. It is a good-size pile of oak logs saturated with starter fluid.

Initially, the fire is so hot that the group can barely stand around it in a circle without turning their faces away. They chant "Om" as they surround the fire.

"I can't believe I'm doing this," says Rev. Anne Gillis, the minister of the Connection Church, which is sponsoring the firewalk.

"I've known about firewalking for a long time and I've wanted to do it, but I'm not sure I'll walk."

No one else is, either. And although Mrs. Thomas promises that their lives will be changed if they cross the coals, she says it is more important to "follow your inner guidance. And if that says, 'Don't walk,' then don't walk."

For those who get a different message, however, she demonstrates exactly how to cross the coals safely - eyes raised, right fist lifted, feet moving quickly but no running, and the firewalker repeating, "cool moss, cool moss."

"That's what you want it to feel like," said Mrs. Thomas, who five minutes later strode quickly across the coals without injury.

At the far end, a man with a garden hose sprayed her feet. Then, she joined the circle and waited for the first volunteer - Rev. Gillis - to stand in front of the coals, take several deep breaths, and step off across the cherry-red pit.

One by one, the firewalkers, including Mrs. Thomas' 12-year-old daughter, Julie, stand at the edge of the pit, close their eyes, convince themselves they can walk on fire and, in most cases, go. On the other side, they shout, cheer, laugh, cry and accept the congratulations of their fellow walkers.

"I've only known two people who were severely burned," Mrs. Thomas says. "They tried to pretend they were not afraid, became misaligned and got burned. No one is totally free of fear. I've done it more than 120 times and I still have a trace of fear."

Mrs. Thomas' daughter had more than a trace. She was crying when she reached the other.

"I don't think I got burned," she said, shaking, "but I was real, real scared. I did it when I was 9, but I wasn't this scared."

Karen King, who faced the coals four times without being able to cross them, was the last firewalker.

She clasped her hands, hung her head, bent double at the waist, prayed, agonized, retreated and wept.

"Every time I get ready to go, a voice whispers, what if," she said. "I'm scared to death. It's as if every fear I ever had was right there in front of me.

"I'm always messing things up. And I kept thinking - I don't want to mess this up for sure.

"I don't want to get burned. I didn't think I could do it until Christina told me that if my baby (a 5-month-old boy) was at the other end of the fire and needed me, I could do it. I knew then I could."

Suddenly, Mrs. King, who with her husband runs a wholesale souvenir business, was on the other side of the fire, tearful and delighted.

"Oh," she said, "I did it, didn't I? Didn't I?"

Afterwards, the firewalkers said they wanted proof that they'd actually walked on beds of coals.

Why can't we have a Firewalkers T-shirt, they wonder. Otherwise, who'd believe it?

Grateful Acknowledgement:
Reprint of this article is made
possible by permission from
The Commercial Appeal

d

The Aquarian Network

ARIZONA

Dr. Frank Alper
Arizona Metaphysical Society
3336 N. 32d Street
Phoenix 85018
(602) 956-1676

Dr. Hirindra Singh
Peace at Home Int'l Foundation
P. O. Box 44227
Phoenix 85064
(602) 776-0942

Dr. Marilyn Wells
Osteopathy
14435 N. 7th St., Suite 300
Phoenix 85022
(602) 863-1951

ARKANSAS

Ron & Janet Loerop
Certified Hypnotherapists
Arkansas Center for
Hypnosis and Regression
10 Shady Hills Drive
Royal, AR 71968
(501) 767-1048

Herb Pablo
Integrative Rebirthing/Counseling
Stress Management
P. O. Box 2751
West Memphis, AR 72303
(501) 732-1238

Rev. Frances G. Varner
Rebirther-Astrologer-Counselor
1901 West Stone Street
Fayetteville, AR 72701
(501) 443-1849

CALIFORNIA

Self-Realization Fellowship
Mother Center
3880 San Rafael Avenue
Los Angeles 90065
(213) 225-2471

Susan Baumann, BA, MT
Somato Emotional
Release Therapy
1408 Stratford Court
Del Mar 92014
(619) 269-0682

CALIFORNIA continued

Cliff & Patricia Mikkelson
Awake & Ready Times
1106 Second St., Ste 107
Encinitas, CA 92024
(619) 942-2959

Dr. Sonia N. Powers
Psychologist/Rebirther/Seminars
415 M Ave. Pico, Suite 200
San Clemente, CA 92672
(714) 498-1818

COLORADO

Steven K. Gehrke
Miracles Happen/Vivation Professional
711 S. Granby Circle
Aurora, CO 80012
(303 751-0502

GEORGIA

Barbra Barber
Seven Rays Studio
Spiritual Art & Workshops
315 Magnolia St.
St. Simons Island, GA 31522
(912) 638-4975

MINNESOTA

Justin & Theresa O'Brien
Yes International!
P. O. Box 75032
St. Paul 55175
(612) 293-8094

MISSISSIPPI

Joanne Cusack
Kirlian Photography
Authority on Human Aura
P.O.Box 53
Sherman, MS 38869
(601) 840-1069

MISSOURI

Pat Murrell, AVP MSW
Mothersource
Psychiatric Social Worker
Box 23305, St. Louis, MO 63156
187 W. 19 St., Alton, IL 62002
(618) 462-4051

212

OKLAHOMA

Carol W. Parrish
Light of Christ
Community Church
  Seminary
  Retreats
  New Age Community
P. O. Box 1274
Tahlequah 74465
(918) 456-3421

TENNESSEE

John Colton
  Win/Win Attorney
1440 Poplar
Memphis 38105
(901) 523-8005

Sharon D. Gary
  Psychological Services
  of Memphis
2714 Union Ave. Ext. #224
Memphis 38112
(901) 323-5585

Betty S. Hutto
  Riversong Life
  Improvement Programs
147 Jefferson, Suite 1000
Memphis 38103-2240
(901) 525-7001 728-6288

Nexus: A Place to Grow
Life Patterning Center
Route 1, Box 352A
Collierville 38017
(901) 853-1784

Sara Reynolds
  Intuitive Counseling
5876 Sun Cove, #2
Memphis 38134
(901) 373-3748

TENNESSEE continued

Christina Thomas

Christina Thomas   umming
977 Seminole Trail   :e
Suite 308
Charlottesville, VA 22901

Carol Risher
  Intuitive Counseling
  Rebirthing
746 North Auburndale
Memphis 38107
(901) 274-4750

Nathan Hoffman
Writing Resource Center
  Creative Writing , Graphics
1835 Union Ave., Suite 111
Memphis 38104
(901) 274-7267

TEXAS

Allen Hahn
  Intuitive Counsel
P. O. Box 1175
Kemah 77565
(713) 333-3040

VIRGINIA

Barbara Begeman
Rainbow Mountain Retreats
  Vibrational Healing
  Lecturer/Astrologer
Star Route 1, Box 67
Montebello 24464
(703) 377-6709

WASHINGTON

Sondra Holt
  Secrets of Powerful Sales
31707 41st Ave East
Eatonville 98328
(206) 847-8700

Recommended Reading

Autobiography of a Yogi, Paramahansa Yogananda

Scientific Healing Affirmations, Paramahansa Yogananda

Being a Christ, Ann and Peter Meyer

Cosmic Consciousness, Richard Maurice Bucke

Joy's Way, W. Brugh Joy, M. D.

Living in the Light, Shakti Gawain

Guiding Your Self Into a Spiritual Reality, Peggy Burkan

One Minute Wisdom, Anthony deMello, S. J.

Rebirthing, the Science of Enjoying All of Your Life, Phil Laut and Jim Leonard

Rebirthing Made Easy, Collin Sisson

Loving Relationships, Sondra Ray

Open Heart Therapy, Bob Mandel

Your Maximum Mind, Herbert Benson, M. D.

Ecstasy is a New Frequency, Christina Griscom

Hands of Light, Barbara Ann Brennan

The Secret Life of the Unborn Child, Thomas Verny, M. D.

Siddhartha, Herman Hesse

Starseed Transmissions by Raphael (through Ken Carey)

Do What You Love, the Money Will Follow, M. Sinetar, Ph.D.

You Can Have It All, Arnold Patent

Healing the Child Within, Charles L. Whitfield, M.D.

Living the Infinite Way, Ralph Waldo Trine

ORDER FORM

Chela Publications
977 Seminole Trail, Suite 308
Charlottesville, VA 22901 • USA
(804) 961-2960

Please send me the following:

____SECRETS	Book	$9.95
____SECRETS	Audio Cassette	9.95
____REBIRTHING: HEAL YOUR LIFE	Audio Cassette	9.95
____STOP SMOKING THE EASY WAY - Audio Cassette		9.95

Name:_____

Address:_____

_____ ZIP: _____

VISA/MASTERCARD #_____Exp.Date_____

Signature_____
Shipping: $1 for the first item and 75c for each additional item.
_____ I can't wait 3-4 weeks for Book Rate. Here is $3 per book for Air Mail.
_____ Please send me your Newsletter and Schedule of Workshops.

The beautiful Cover Art is "BLUE DRIFT" @1987 by Southern California Artist Thomas Canny. It is now available as a Poster directly from Tom: "Blue Drift" printed on Certified 100% Archival Paper, paper size of 20"x25" and an image size of 15"x20". It is a Limited Edition of 450 plus 50 Artist Proofs.

Signed and numbered $85.00
Signed Artist Proof $95.00

Send check/ money order plus $6 shipping to:

THOMAS CANNY STUDIO, P.O.Box 1462, Temple City, CA 91780-7462

In California, add tax.

Notes

Notes

ORDER FORM

Chela Publications
977 Seminole Trail, Suite 308
Charlottesville, VA 22901 • USA
(804) 961-2960

Please send me the following:

____SECRETS   Book $9.95

____SECRETS   Audio Cassette   9.95

____REBIRTHING: HEAL YOUR LIFE   Audio Cassette   9.95

____STOP SMOKING THE EASY WAY - Audio Cassette   9.95

Name:_____

Address:_____

_____ ZIP: _____

VISA/MASTERCARD #_____Exp.Date_____

Signature_____
Shipping: $1 for the first item and 75c for each additional item.
_____ I can't wait 3-4 weeks for Book Rate. Here is $3 per <u>book</u> for Air Mail.
_____ Please send me your Newsletter and Schedule of Workshops.

The beautiful Cover Art is "BLUE DRIFT"@1987 by Southern California Artist Thomas Canny. It is now available as a Poster directly from Tom: "Blue Drift" printed on Certified 100% Archival Paper, paper size of 20"x25" and an image size of 15"x20". It is a Limited Edition of 450 plus 50 Artist Proofs.

        Signed and numbered $85.00

        Signed Artist Proof $95.00

Send check/ money order plus $6 shipping to:

THOMAS CANNY STUDIO, P.O.Box 1462, Temple City, CA 91780-7462

In California, add tax.

WHAT PEOPLE ARE SAYING ABOUT THIS BOOK . . .

"We are greater than we think. There is untapped spiritual, mental and physical energy available to heal and strengthen us. SECRETS is a no-nonsense, down-to-earth and accurate guide to these inner capacities."

> *Dr. John Culkin, Director*
> *Center for Understanding Media*
> *New York City*

"Powerful insights . . . I have experienced healing and a sense of wholeness I never knew before. Must reading for anyone serious about personal aliveness and growth!"

> *Sharon D. Gary, Director*
> *Psychological Services*

"Created a powerful turning point for me, giving me a sense of connectedness and helping me to be in touch with my Higher Self. My life is filled with love and understanding now."

> *John Colton, Attorney*

". . . brought me face-to-face with the jarring, inescapable reality that I am capable of accomplishments which are way beyond my ability to explain!"

> *William Thomas, Staff Reporter*
> *The Commercial Appeal*

"Provides clear tools for transformation, bridging in a direct manner between mind and spiritual principles - no easy task. Christina handles this delicate process with sensitivity."

> *Carol W. Parrish-Harra, Author*
> *Messengers of Hope*